Dave Maynard's
SOUPS, STEWS, &
CASSEROLES

Dave Maynard's
SOUPS, STEWS,&
CASSEROLES

*☞And Many Other
Tried and True Recipes for
Chilis, Chowders, and
Other Hearty Fare*

Edited by DAVE MAYNARD
Assistant Editor: DENISE C. RUSSO

ST. MARTIN'S PRESS · NEW YORK

Design by Mina Greenstein

Library of Congress Cataloging in Publication Data

Maynard, Dave, 1929–
    Dave Maynard's soups, stews, and casseroles.

    1. Soups.   2. Stews.   3. Casserole cookery.
I. Title.
TX757.M39   1984   641.8'13   84-11723
ISBN 0-312-18359-3
ISBN 0-312-18360-7 (pbk.)

First Edition
10 9 8 7 6 5 4 3 2 1

To Ruth—
who nearly drove me crazy—
but got this done.

Contents

Foreword

All things considered, I'm an extremely lucky person—in more ways than one. I've had a good education, a large, healthy family, an exciting and challenging job, and been able to travel extensively, and as you see by the cover, I'm very handsome. I've had many thrills, worldwide. Here're ten:

1. Walked the great wall of China
2. Rode a nasty, rotten camel around the great pyramid of Giza
3. Secretly snapped (by armpit camera), a shot of Checkpoint Charley going from West to East Berlin. (That's the dangerous way.)
4. Marveled at the *David* in Florence, the Sistine Chapel in Rome, the Louvre, and the Prado
5. Was part of a $458 dinner in Hong Kong (Peninsula Hotel)
6. Outdrank a young Russian guy in Leningrad who was obviously trying to get me bombed (Lord, was I sick for two days!)
7. Have spoken to:
   a. two presidents
   b. four men running for the presidency
   c. too many governors and senators to even mention
   d. countless movie and recording stars

8. Have
   a. fought (and hit) a world boxing champion (Marvin Hagler)
   b. almost hit a home run in Fenway Park
   c. played golf with Arnold Palmer
   d. played tennis with Bobby Riggs
   e. played hockey and basketball in Boston Garden
   f. skied Tuckermans Ravine in April
9. Had a straight-razor shave on the Isle of Crete in one of the many shave shops right on the dock. (Sit-lather-whip-whip-whip-whip-done. All in twenty-two seconds. It's some thrill, all right.)
10. BUT, the biggest thrill of all hit me like 904.97 kilograms of bricks (the metric system is coming, friends—be ready!), in San Francisco.

There I was, somewhere in the Embarcadero, browsing idly in a bookstore. As usual, I drifted to the cookbook section, knowing that I'd never see a copy of the first Tried and True cookbook and wishing it were not so. After all, who would know about me and this book that had sold so many more copies (by triple) than I'd ever expected. All of a sudden, I saw the nose, that huge red beak, and I knew San Franciscans weren't so dumb after all. I must admit, it was a trifle embarrassing when a salesgirl frittered over and asked me if I saw anything I liked. I said well, yes (hoping she'd see the author's pride on my face), and she said, "You seem to be a little mesmerized. You've been just standing there for a half an hour." Boy, was she wrong. I certainly hadn't been just standing there. What I'd done was to neatly rearrange the display so that the *Dave Maynard's Tried and True Secret Family Recipe Cookbook* was more prominent than Julia Child or James Beard.

Truthfully, in my wildest dreams, never would I imagine that first cookbook would be the success it has been. When it was done, I tried to be objective, tasting and testing every day. But, in truth, I thought it was a pretty interesting volume. No need for the Rombauers to get nervous, you understand, but still a different, honest cookbook that didn't cost too much.

By the way, I had the occasion to lunch with James Beard one afternoon during his national tour with Marion Cunningham, who did such a glorious job on the *New Fanny Farmer Cookbook.* He turned to me, not the least bit distracted by my obvious ogling, and said softly, "I understand you've done a cookbook— I'd like to read it." Just what the world's record is for the ninety-yard dash is, I don't know. I *do* know it was set or equaled that day in Newton, Massachusetts, two years ago.

Sorry, I can't think of the name of a wonderful lady in Rochester, New York, who has over three hundred cookbooks in her collection and who wrote and said ours was one of the very best.

Notice the pronoun—*ours.* That's what it is. A book of *our* recipes. Shared treasures handed down from generation to generation. Tested and tasted by thousands in good times and bad. You know, sometimes in the kitchen, when tasting an end result, I've become a little daydreamy. I can actually see and hear a family being called into dinner on a cold winter's night, sitting down to big steaming bowls of fish chowder or old-fashioned beef stew, with big chunks of everything in it. Good Lord, it's no wonder many people still say grace before dining. A good meal sure can change your attitude from mean to jolly and make your perspectives really brighten—so:

Here it is, Book Number 2—
May it lift your spirits a notch or two.
Hope you read and use it as others will do—
Remember, every single recipe is Tried and True.

DAVE MAYNARD

Dave Maynard's
SOUPS, STEWS, &
CASSEROLES

SOUPS

☞ IGNORING the soup course in New England on a nice, cold, crisp day is very tacky, gauche, and obtuse. I mean, it just isn't done. People might think you're from someplace uncivilized, like New Jersey or Oklahoma, maybe. Just kidding, folks. Actually, the best soups I ever had, night after night, were served to me at the Inn at Pinehurst, North Carolina. I order soup everywhere I travel, although I know that in many cases it's a good place to hide stuff.

Here are some Hall-of-Famers:

1. *Cream of Bell Pepper,* Zachary's in the Colonnade, Boston
2. *Gaspacho,* Laurent Café, New York City
3. *Lentil,* Bones, Atlanta
4. *Chicken Broth,* Akasaka Misono, Tokyo, Japan
5. *Cream of Chicken,* Peninsula Hotel, Hong Kong
6. *Phyllis Diller's Garbage Soup,* my house
7. *Clam Chowder,* one hundred places in New England

At last count, I had received over three hundred recipes for fish chowder. Many are alike in several respects. Most start with salt pork, and that made me happy cuz I was learnt that way. (I wouldn't want any of my Massachusetts friends to know that I *also* like *Manhattan* clam chowder with tomatoes in it. My dad used to make it a lot during those fearful days of the Depression. We lived on Long Island Sound; clams were free and plentiful, and he did chop them real small—you know how clams look to a kid when they're whole!

Sometimes it's hard to be humble, so I'll honestly tell you that I make the best fish chowder in the world, thanks to Mary and Frank Texeira of Buzzards Bay, Massachusetts—two people who, like most Portuguese, love the ocean and everything in it. They were the folks who patiently showed me the difference between fish chowder and pieces of fish in hot milk.

As I said in the first book, you must put all of the fish into the pot *except* the fillets. Fins, tails, heads, gills, *everything,* or there'll be a lot of blah in the soup bowls. The nice white chunks of fish are added just before serving. And while I'm at it, why do so many people put their potatoes in so early? So they can get nice and mushy? I'd better stop, I'm getting vicious!

If Phyllis Diller ever gets a copy of this book (and I'll make sure she does), she might remember me as the pleasant young man who emceed the show at Fort Devens, Massachusetts, very early in her career and proudly took her back to a nineteen-room Victorian ogre that I was restoring in Lexington, near the John Hancock House. I remember it well. She said, "My God, I've always wanted a big old house and I'll get one." She sure did—about one year later. She made garbage soup for us on television, nearly took the roof off my mouth that afternoon. Someone had cutesied it up with Tabasco.

Cream soups are my favorite. Guess that's why I chose so many for the book. Too bad some folks don't go a step further with their soup making. Cream of Barley, Leek and Watercress, Pumpkin, anything green. I've taken to saving all kinds of cooking waters—spinach, beet greens, etc.—freezing and saving. I plop them into whatever soup seems compatible. Don't you hate to pour vitamins and minerals down the kitchen sink?

Well, happy blending—and by the way, thanks for all those pea soup recipes (each claiming, "This is the best you've ever tasted"). I can understand your chauvinism, but there's one thing you must know, *I* make the best.

By the way, if you like pea soup so much that you are driven to using a package of instant soup mix, use half beer and half water and throw in some frozen or fresh peas, as well as a little diced fresh carrot.

You do preheat your soup bowls, don't you? I thought so.

PEPPER POT SOUP
(Caribbean)

2 pounds stewing beef, cut into 1-inch cubes
½ pound salt beef or pork, diced
2 quarts water
1 box (10 ounces) frozen okra, thawed, chopped in ½-inch pieces
2 small green peppers, seeded and chopped

2 boxes (10 ounces each) frozen chopped spinach, thawed
2 scallions, chopped
1 pound yams, pared and cut in ½-inch chunks
½ teaspoon dried thyme
1 clove garlic, finely chopped
Salt and pepper to taste

☐Cook all the meat, partially covered, in 2 quarts of water over low heat for about 1 hour, skimming the surface occasionally. Add okra, green peppers, spinach, and scallions, and simmer for 15 minutes. Add yams, thyme, garlic, and salt and pepper; cook until yams are cooked, about 30 minutes. If too thick, add more water.

Makes 8 to 10 servings.

Doris Wingood
Burlington, Massachusetts

Dave's Note: Different and quite delicious. I would use fresh spinach.

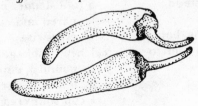

PORTUGUESE SOUP

1 pound yellow-eyed beans,
  soaked overnight in
  water to cover
1 pound stew beef, cut into
  small pieces
Flour
Vegetable oil
1 pound linguica or
  chorizos

1 can (16 ounces) tomatoes
2 medium onions, chopped
2 cloves garlic, chopped
  fine
1 large bay leaf
Salt and pepper to taste
1 small head cabbage,
  shredded

☐Rinse and boil beans in enough water to cover; cook until almost tender. Meanwhile, sauté lightly floured stew beef in vegetable oil. Add to beans in kettle and simmer for 30 minutes. Add sliced sausage and tomatoes and continue to cook, adding onion, garlic, and bay leaf. Cook until meat is tender, adding enough water to make a thick soup. Season with salt and pepper to taste. Add shredded cabbage during the last half hour of cooking.

Evelyn Klassen
New Ipswich, New Hampshire

CHUNKY BORSCHT

4 beef shanks, each about 1
  inch thick (approximately
  2½ pounds)
5 cups water
2 tablespoons lemon
  juice
3 medium onions, halved
1 can (6 ounces) tomato
  paste
½ teaspoon sugar
Salt to taste

6 beets, each about 2
  inches in diameter,
  pared and cut into
  quarters
6 to 8 slender carrots,
  pared and cut in half
  crosswise
1 head cabbage (about 1½
  pounds), cored and cut
  into 6 wedges
1 cup sour cream

☐In a 6- to 8-quart kettle, cook shanks, covered, in 1 cup of the water over medium-high heat to draw juices out of meat (allow about 30 minutes). Uncover and boil until liquid evaporates, turning the meat as needed to brown. Remove from heat and add lemon juice and 2 more cups of water. Scrape pan to loosen brown bits. Set onions on top of meat. Cover and simmer on medium heat until meat pulls easily from the bones, about 1½ hours.

Lift out onions and meat and set aside. In a pan, stir together remaining 2 cups water, the tomato paste, sugar, salt to taste, and beets; set the beef shanks and onions, then carrots, on top. Cover and simmer until beets are tender when pierced, about 40 minutes. Set cabbage wedges on top of carrots; cover and simmer until cabbage turns bright green and is tender-crisp when pierced, about 15 minutes longer.

To serve, lift out cabbage and arrange on a warm serving platter, then arrange carrots, onions, beef, and beets alongside. Put pan juices and sour cream into individual serving dishes and offer for spooning over portions of stew.

Makes 4 to 6 servings.

Dave's

COUNTRY SUPPER SOUP

2 pounds beef chuck, cut in 6 pieces
Salt and pepper to taste
2 tablespoons vegetable oil
2½ quarts water
1 onion, chopped
1 cup sliced celery
½ cup chopped fresh parsley

1 package (10 ounces) frozen mixed vegetables
½ small cabbage, cored and shredded
4 to 6 small potatoes, peeled
1 can (6 ounces) tomato paste

☐Sprinkle chuck with salt and pepper to taste. In a Dutch oven, brown beef in oil on medium-high heat. Add water, onion, celery, parsley, and 1½ tablespoons salt. Bring to a boil, skimming as necessary, then reduce heat and simmer for 1½ hours. Add remaining vegetables and the tomato paste. Simmer for 45 minutes or longer, until potatoes are tender.

Makes 6 servings.

Martin Lescowitch
Weston, Pennsylvania

MEATBALL SOUP
(Albondigas Soup)

1 tablespoon vegetable oil	½ pound ground beef
2 tablespoons minced onion	3 tablespoons soft fresh bread crumbs
1 clove garlic, minced	2 tablespoons cooked rice
1 can (8 ounces) tomato sauce	1 egg
4 cups water	½ teaspoon salt
2 beef bouillon cubes	Dash of pepper

☐In a saucepan, heat oil and sauté onion and garlic until brown. Add tomato sauce, water, and bouillon cubes. Bring to a boil. Meanwhile, combine beef, bread crumbs, rice, egg, salt, and pepper in a bowl. Shape into 1-inch meatballs, approximately 18 to 20. Drop carefully into soup, cover, and cook over low heat for 25 minutes.

Makes 1½ quarts.

Joyce Fontaine
Georgetown, Massachusetts

MEATBALL SOUP WITH ESCAROLE
AND PARSLEY BREAD SQUARES

Some people make this soup with the small Italian macaroni called pastina, but I prefer bread squares, as I think they're really unusual. Also, I usually remove the cooked chicken and use it for chicken salad or sandwiches, since the recipe already includes meatballs. However, the chicken meat could be chopped up and used in place of the meatballs if you prefer. Hope you like it.

4 quarts water
1 chicken (2 to 3 pounds)
1 small beef short rib
1 can (28 ounces) tomatoes
2 stalks celery with leaves,
   chopped
1 onion, chopped
5 carrots, pared
2 chicken bouillon cubes
1 beef bouillon cube
1 bouquet garni (parsley,
   thyme, bay leaf, tied in
   cheesecloth)

Salt and freshly ground
   pepper
2 bunches escarole, washed
   and coarsely chopped
1½ pounds ground lean
   beef
¼ cup plus 1 tablespoon
   grated Parmesan cheese
2 eggs
Parsley Bread Squares
   (recipe follows)

☐Combine the water, whole chicken, beef rib, tomatoes, celery, onion, 1 whole carrot, bouillon cubes, bouquet garni, and salt and pepper to taste in a large stockpot. Bring to a boil over high heat, skimming as necessary. Reduce the heat and simmer, partially covered, for 2 to 2½ hours, adding more water if necessary. Remove from heat and let cool slightly. Strain mixture through a cheesecloth-lined strainer into a large bowl. Repeat. Skin the chicken and discard the bones; chop the meat or tear into shreds. Set aside. Discard the beef rib and vegetables. Let the broth cool completely. Skim the fat from the surface.

Bring a large saucepan of water to a fast boil. Add the escarole and cook, uncovered, for 5 minutes. Drain. Combine the ground beef, the ¼ cup Parmesan cheese, ½ teaspoon salt, and ½ teaspoon pepper in a large bowl and mix well. Shape into 1-inch meatballs. Bring the reserved broth to a boil over medium heat. Add the meatballs and cook, uncovered, for 10 minutes. Chop the remaining 4 carrots and stir into the soup, along with the escarole. Continue cooking for 10 minutes. Beat the eggs with remaining 1 tablespoon Parmesan in a small bowl. Add to the boiling soup and continue cooking, stirring constantly with a fork, for 5 minutes. Remove from the heat and stir in the chopped chicken and Parsley Bread Squares. Serve immediately.

Makes 10 to 12 servings.

Parsley Bread Squares

4 eggs
½ cup grated Parmesan cheese
¼ cup chopped fresh parsley
½ teaspoon salt

½ teaspoon freshly ground pepper
½ cup (or more) all-purpose flour
¼ cup plus 1 tablespoon vegetable oil

☐Beat eggs, cheese, parsley, salt, and pepper in a large bowl until well blended. Add flour, 1 tablespoon at a time, mixing well after each addition (the mixture should be thick; add more flour, 1 teaspoon at a time, if necessary).

Heat the oil in a heavy 10-inch skillet (preferably nonstick) over high heat. Pour in the batter, spreading it to the sides of the skillet with a spatula. Cook until browned on bottom, about 3 minutes. Turn over and continue cooking until browned. Transfer to paper towels and let cool. Cut into small squares.

Marilyn Sandonato
North Scituate, Massachusetts

Dave's Note: I like to add garlic, a little or a lot, depending on my mood, to the meatballs.

OXTAIL SOUP

1 oxtail
1 tablespoon butter
1 large onion, diced
6 cups beef stock
1 carrot, pared and thinly
 sliced
1 stalk celery, thinly sliced
1 bouquet garni (1 sprig
 fresh thyme, 2 sprigs
 fresh parsley, 1 bay leaf,
 tied together)

½ cup chopped fresh or
 canned tomatoes
1 cup claret
1 tablespoon Worces-
 tershire sauce
6 peppercorns, crushed
Salt

☐Wash oxtail well and split it in small joints. Melt butter in a saucepan and add pieces of tail. When meat begins to brown add chopped onion, frying until the onion is deep gold. Add stock, carrot, celery, bouquet garni, chopped tomatoes, and claret. Season with Worcestershire sauce, crushed peppercorns, and salt to taste and bring to a boil, skimming as necessary. Cover and place in a 300°F oven for 8 hours.

When ready to serve, remove the herbs. Separate the meat from the bone and discard the bone. Serve a little of the meat in each bowl of soup.

Makes 6 servings.

Esther H. Thompson
West Newton, Massachusetts

Dave's Note: If you can't get oxtail, you can substitute with beef knuckle or shin bones, approximately 1½ pounds.

BEEF SOUP
(*Brodo di Manzo*)

1½ pounds beef chuck or
   brisket
1 pound beef soup bone
   with marrow
2 or 3 tablespoons chopped
   canned tomato or 1
   large fresh tomato,
   peeled and chopped
2 whole carrots, pared and
   cut in 2-inch strips

1 large onion, quartered
2 stalks celery with leaves,
   cut in 2-inch strips
2 sprigs fresh parsley,
   chopped
Salt and pepper
½ pound pastina or 1
   cup rice
Grated Romano or
   Parmesan cheese

☐ Place meat and bone in a soup kettle and cover with cold water. Bring slowly to a boil. Skim fat off top with a spoon. Add vegetables and parsley to the meat and season with salt and pepper. Cover kettle and cook slowly over low heat until meat is tender, about 2 hours. Remove meat and vegetables from the soup and strain broth through sieve or colander. Return broth and vegetables to soup kettle. Discard bone and return meat to soup. Add pastina and continue to cook for 8 to 12 minutes. (If you prefer rice, cook for 18 minutes, or until tender.) Serve with grated cheese.
Makes 8 servings.

Mrs. William E. Cipriano
Cranston, Rhode Island

LITTLE SCOTIA BARLEY SOUP

My mother served this at least once a week as our lunch soup when we came home from school cold and hungry, having walked or run about two miles for the nourishing soup she always had waiting for us. Later on in 1948 she opened a tearoom called "Little Scotia," meaning Little Scotland, the land of our birth. My mother is ninety-one years old and, unfortunately, is no longer able to do her own cooking, but we all have fond memories of her wonderful food.

2 pounds hough (Scottish
    name for shin of beef)
1 pound lamb neck
1 onion, chopped
Several stalks parsley
1 stalk celery
1 teaspoon salt
¼ teaspoon pepper
Dash of cayenne
2 cups finely grated carrots

2 cups diced carrots
2 cups diced onions
2 cups diced celery
1 can (16 ounces) peas
1 can (16 ounces) green
    beans
½ cup barley, soaked in
    1 cup water for ½ hour
¼ cup chopped parsley

☐Brown together the lamb and beef. Place in a large kettle with 12 cups of water, 1 chopped onion, several stalks of parsley (reserve the leaves for later use), 1 stalk celery, 1 teaspoon salt, ¼ teaspoon pepper, and a dash of cayenne. Simmer until the meat is tender. Strain and remove meat from the bones and set aside. Discard vegetables. Return the stock to kettle and add the remaining ingredients. Simmer for about 2 hours and then return the meat to the kettle. Simmer for an additional hour and adjust seasonings. Cool and refrigerate. Remove hardened fat and discard. It freezes very well since there are no potatoes in the soup.

Note: Finely grated carrots are essential to the flavor of the soup.

Margaret L. Yells
Seneca Falls, New York

SOUTH OF THE BORDER SOUP

1 pound ground beef
1 medium onion, chopped
Salt and pepper
2 stalks celery, chopped
    (about ¾ cup)

1 large carrot, pared
    and sliced (about
    1½ cups)
1 can (16 ounces) peeled
    tomatoes, undrained

1 zucchini, sliced (about 1
   cup)
1 cup water
¾ cup fresh or frozen
   corn kernels

1 tablespoon chili powder
1 beef bouillon cube or 1
   teaspoon powdered beef
   bouillon

☐ Cook beef in a large saucepan over medium heat, breaking into chunks, until partially browned. Add onion and salt and pepper to taste and cook, stirring, until the meat is cooked through. Blend in remaining ingredients. Increase heat to medium-high and bring to a boil, then reduce heat to low and simmer, covered, until vegetables are tender, about 30 minutes. Ladle into bowls and serve immediately.

Makes 4 to 6 servings.

Dave's

MANASTRA

1 tablespoon salt
1 large bunch broccoli or 2
   packages (10 ounces
   each) frozen broccoli
1 large head cauliflower or
   2 packages (10 ounces
   each) frozen cauliflower
1 pound peas, shelled
   weight, or 2 packages
   (10 ounces each) frozen
   peas
Any other leftover
   vegetables, except for
   beets

1 pound elbow macaroni
1 medium onion, chopped
2 tablespoons vegetable oil
2 pounds ground beef
2 cans (16 ounces each)
   stewed tomatoes
Pepper to taste
2 teaspoons sugar
Pinch of baking soda
1 teaspoon dried oregano

☐ Add the salt to 5 to 6 quarts of water and bring to a boil. Break the fresh broccoli and cauliflower into florets and add with peas and any other vegetable of your choice to boiling water; cook, uncovered, for about 3 minutes. Add macaroni and cook for 9 to 12 minutes.

Meanwhile, in a frying pan, sauté chopped onion in hot oil until softened, then add the ground beef and brown well. Drain this mixture on paper toweling and add to soup, along with stewed tomatoes, pepper, sugar, baking soda, and oregano. Let soup simmer for 5 to 10 minutes before serving.

Makes about 20 servings.

E. Egan

HAMBURG SOUP

I really wish I had an interesting story connected with this recipe, but it actually comes from a diet workshop class. It is a flexible recipe you can add to or subtract from, but, as printed, it is a low-calorie soup that makes a delicious meal for the whole family.

2 pounds ground beef
6 cups tomato juice
1 cup stewed tomatoes
1 bay leaf
1 tablespoon garlic powder
2 cups chopped celery
1 cup sliced pared carrots
2 teaspoons dried basil
2 teaspoons dried oregano
2 teaspoons onion flakes

Salt to taste
1 cup canned mushrooms,
     drained
1 tablespoon
     Worcestershire sauce
2 cups French-style green
     beans
2 cups thinly sliced
     cabbage

☐ Brown beef in a large saucepan; drain well. Combine all the other ingredients and add to beef. Simmer, partially covered, for 2 hours.

Makes 8 to 10 servings.

Mrs. Shirley Leighton
Randolph, Massachusetts

SHINBONE SOUP

This really hits the spot on a cold winter night. Serve with thick slices of Italian or French bread in deep, old-fashioned bowls.

1 meaty shinbone
4 quarts water
1 can (16 ounces) tomato purée
1 very large onion (or 2 medium onions), chopped
1 bunch carrots, pared and chopped

1 bunch celery with tops, trimmed and chopped
Salt and pepper to taste
Thin ribbon macaroni, pastina, or soup macaroni

☐ Place shinbone in a large (6- to 8-quart) kettle with 4 quarts of water. Add the tomato purée, onion, and the cut-up *leaves* of celery. Cover and bring to a boil; lower heat and simmer for about 2 hours. Add the chopped carrots and let simmer for 1 hour longer, checking to see when carrots are tender (you don't want them mushy). If the liquid boils down, add more water. Add chopped celery and continue to simmer until celery is tender. Remove meat and let cool. Skim fat from top. Add seasonings to taste. Cut up meat in chunks; discard bone and return the meat to soup. Add a big handful of pasta (or as much as you want). Simmer a few minutes longer, but don't let things get over-cooked.

I find that if I add macaroni to soup when I remove meat for cooling and turn the heat off, the macaroni will cook just right in the hot liquid for about 10 to 15 minutes.

Makes 12 servings.

Mrs. Margaret Warshaw
Braintree, Massachusetts

Dave's Note: You may want to cook the macaroni in a separate pan, slightly undercooking. Then add it to the soup. I did.

CREAM OF REUBEN SOUP

½ cup beef broth
½ cup chicken broth
¼ cup coarsely chopped
  celery
¼ cup coarsely chopped
  onion
¼ cup coarsely chopped
  green pepper
1 tablespoon cornstarch
  dissolved in 2
  tablespoons of water

1 cup coarsely chopped
  corned beef
1 cup chopped Swiss
  cheese
¾ cup sauerkraut,
  drained and rinsed
¼ cup butter
2 cups half-and-half
Chopped fresh chives

☐Combine broths, celery, onion, and green pepper in a large saucepan and bring to a boil over high heat. Reduce heat and simmer, uncovered, until the vegetables are crisp-tender, about 5 minutes. Add dissolved cornstarch and continue cooking until soup thickens. Remove from the heat and stir in corned beef, Swiss cheese, and drained sauerkraut, blending well.

Melt butter in a large double-boiler over medium heat. Stir in half-and-half. Add soup and blend until smooth. Heat through over simmering water but do not boil. Garnish with chives to serve.

Makes 8 servings.

Dave's

Dave's Note: Be sure to drain the kraut well.

VEGETABLE BEEF SOUP (STEW?)

3 pounds boneless beef, cut
  in 1-inch cubes
6 tablespoons vegetable oil
1 cup chopped onion
1 cup chopped green
  pepper

1 cup chopped celery
2 tablespoons chopped
  fresh parsley
1 clove garlic, chopped
1 can (8 ounces) tomato
  sauce

1 cup red wine
2 beef bouillon cubes
1½ tablespoons salt
¼ teaspoon pepper
⅛ teaspoon dried thyme
    leaves
1 bay leaf
2 cups water
6 small potatoes, pared and
    diced

6 medium carrots, sliced
1 cup green beans, canned
    or frozen
1 cup corn, canned or
    frozen
1 tablespoon all-purpose
    flour
2 tablespoons cold water

☐Brown beef cubes well on all sides in hot oil in a large sauce-pan. Remove from pan and set aside. Add chopped onion, green pepper, and celery and sauté for 8 minutes. Return beef to the pan. Add parsley, garlic, tomato sauce, wine, bouillon cubes, salt, pepper, thyme, bay leaf, and water. Bring to a boil, then reduce heat and simmer, covered, for 1¼ hours. Add re-maining vegetables and simmer, covered, for 1 hour longer. Remove from heat and skim off fat. Mix flour with the 2 table-spoons cold water and stir into the pot.

Makes 6 or more servings.

Note: I brown the meat in my pressure cooker according to the directions, and when the pressure drops off I remove the meat and sauté the onion, peppers, and celery.

Kathleen Power
South Hamilton, Massachusetts

COUNTRY BAKED SOUP

Very easy and handy when you want to play some touch football on a Saturday afternoon.

1 cup dried split peas
1 pound boneless lamb,
    trimmed and cut in
    1-inch cubes

1 carrot, pared and diced
1 onion, minced
1 teaspoon salt
Generous grind of pepper

☐Pick over peas. Cover with cold water and soak overnight.
Preheat oven to 300°F.

Drain peas and place in a bean pot. Add remaining ingredients
and stir lightly. Add enough cold water to cover mixture entirely.
Cover and bake for 3 to 4 hours, or until mixture is well cooked.
Add boiling water during cooking if soup becomes too thick.
Makes 6 servings.

Dave's

BOOYA

3 pounds beef short ribs
2 pounds boneless beef, cut
in cubes
2 pounds boneless pork,
cut in cubes
2½ pounds soup bones,
split
1½ pounds oxtails
4 large onions, chopped
6 cups fresh parsley sprigs
½ cup dried split peas
½ cup dried lima beans
1 tablespoon chopped
garlic
1½ tablespoons pepper
Salt to taste
1 tablespoon dried oregano

1 tablespoon dried basil
1 tablespoon paprika
1 tablespoon dried savory
1 large head cabbage,
chopped
3 cups diced carrots
3 cups diced rutabaga
1 cup diced green pepper
2 cans (28 ounces each)
tomatoes
2 cans (15 ounces each)
green beans
1 can (17 ounces) peas
1 can (17 ounces) whole
kernel corn
⅓ cup barley

☐In a large kettle, combine meats, bones, onions, parsley, peas,
beans, garlic, and seasonings. Add water to cover. Bring to a boil,
skimming as necessary, then reduce heat, cover, and simmer for
about 5 hours.

Remove meat from bones and return to soup; discard bones.
Skim fat from stock. Add cabbage, carrot, rutabaga, celery, and

green pepper. Simmer, covered, for 1 more hour. Add undrained canned vegetables and simmer for 30 minutes more.
    Makes 14 quarts.

Mr. and Mrs. Rick Rickerman
Chelsea, Minnesota

ARMENIAN YOGURT-BARLEY SOUP

2 large leeks, thoroughly
    washed and sliced
1 medium onion, sliced
1 large stalk celery,
    trimmed and coarsely
    chopped
1 medium carrot, pared
    and coarsely chopped
6 cups water
1 pound lamb shoulder
    with bone
1 cup medium pearl barley,
    rinsed

1 tablespoon salt
½ teaspoon freshly
    ground white pepper
3 tablespoons snipped
    fresh mint or 1
    tablespoon dried mint
    leaves
1 tablespoon unsalted
    butter
1½ to 2 cups plain yogurt
1 egg, beaten

☐Add vegetables to a Dutch oven with water and lamb. Heat over medium-high heat until boiling. Reduce heat and simmer, covered, stirring occasionally, until meat is tender and vegetables are very soft, about 1 hour.
    Strain mixture; return broth and lamb to Dutch oven. Purée vegetables in food processor or blender and return to Dutch oven. Stir in barley, salt, and pepper. Bring to a boil and simmer, covered, stirring occasionally, until barley is tender, about 1 hour. Remove lamb with slotted spoon and shred meat into small pieces. Discard bone and return meat to soup.
    Sauté mint in the butter about 30 seconds. Whisk 1½ cups yogurt and the egg in small bowl. Stir ½ cup of the soup into yogurt mixture. Stir yogurt mixture gradually into soup; heat

over low heat until warm. Add mint, then taste and adjust seasonings with salt, pepper, and remaining yogurt, if desired.
Makes 8 servings.

Dave's

ONION, HAM, AND CHEESE SOUP

I find I only cook from scratch; whether that's good or bad, I'm not sure, but we now raise our own meats and vegetables. Soups are easy and very filling, certainly help to warm you up in a cold, old house. I've only got two "real" recipes for soups—the others are whatever is in the refrigerator at the time—but all are excellent with hot, buttered biscuits.

2 medium potatoes, pared and cut into 1-inch cubes
½ cup boiling water, or as necessary
1 cup chopped onion
3 tablespoons butter
3 tablespoons all-purpose flour

Pepper
3 cups milk
1½ cups chopped cooked ham
1½ cups grated American cheese

☐Cook potatoes in boiling water until tender, about 10 minutes. Drain, reserving the liquid. Add enough of the boiling water to reserved liquid to make 1 cup.

In a large saucepan, cook onion in butter until tender. Blend in flour and a dash of pepper. Add milk and potato water all at once. Cook and stir until it bubbles. Add ham and cheese. Soup is ready as soon as cheese melts.
Makes 8 servings.

Joyce Fontaine
Georgetown, Massachusetts

Editor's Note: For Joyce's other "real" recipe, see page 6.

HAM CHOWDER

2 cups cubed potatoes
4 tablespoons butter
½ cup diced celery
½ cup chopped onion
1 cup cubed ham or
    smoked shoulder
2 tablespoons all-purpose
    flour

4 cups milk
Salt to taste
¼ teaspoon pepper
½ teaspoon chopped
    fresh parsley
Grated cheese of your
    choice

☐ Boil potatoes until almost tender; drain and set aside. Melt butter in a kettle and add celery and onion; sauté. Add ham and cook for 5 minutes more on low heat. Blend flour and milk together and add to kettle, stirring constantly until smooth. Add potatoes and cook for about 7 minutes longer. Season with salt and pepper. Sprinkle each bowl with parsley and pass around grated cheese for those who like it.
   Makes 4 to 6 servings.

Flo Maine
North Reading, Massachusetts

HAM BONE SOUP

1 package (8 ounces) dried
    lima beans
1 package (8 ounces) barley
Bone and shins of ham or
    small piece of ham
2 onions, halved or
    quartered
4 carrots, pared, then
    sliced or diced

3 stalks celery with leaves,
    chopped
4 potatoes, pared and cut
    in quarters
1 can (16 ounces) tomatoes
Salt and pepper
Paprika

☐ Add lima beans and barley to about 4 cups or more of boiling water in soup kettle. When it comes to a second boil, add ham

bone and shins or small pieces of ham. Simmer, partially covered, for about an hour, then add more water and the onions, carrots, celery, potatoes, salt and pepper to taste. Bring to a slow boil for 30 minutes to 1 hour. During the last 15 minutes, add tomatoes and a dash of paprika.
Makes 8 servings.

Mrs. Marilyn Trygar
Old Forge, Pennsylvania

Dave's Note: Basic ham stock–type soup. Watch the salt, as ham itself is probably salty.

ITALIAN SAUSAGE–ZUCCHINI SOUP

1 pound Italian sweet or hot sausage, casings removed
2 large stalks celery, sliced on an angle in ½-inch pieces (about 2 cups)
2 pounds zucchini, sliced
1 cup chopped onion
2 cans (28 ounces each) tomatoes, undrained
1 teaspoon Italian seasoning
2 teaspoons salt
1 teaspoon dried oregano
1 teaspoon sugar
½ teaspoon dried basil
¼ teaspoon garlic powder or 1 clove garlic, crushed
4 cups water
2 green peppers, seeded and cut in ½-inch pieces
½ cup red wine (optional)

☐ Brown sausage; discard excess fat. Add celery and sauté for 10 minutes, stirring occasionally. Add remaining ingredients, except for green peppers and wine. Simmer, covered, 20 minutes. Add green pepper and, if desired, red wine. Cook, covered, another 10 minutes.
Makes 3½ to 4 quarts.

Mrs. Edith Witt
Canton, Massachusetts

ITALIAN SAUSAGE SOUP

1½ pounds mild Italian
 sausage, cut in ½-inch
 pieces
2 cloves garlic, minced
2 large onions, chopped
1 can (28 ounces) Italian
 plum tomatoes, chopped
3 cans (10½ ounces each)
 beef broth
1½ cups dry red wine

3 tablespoons chopped
 fresh parsley
½ teaspoon dried basil
 leaves, crumbled
1 medium green pepper,
 seeded and chopped
3 cups noodles
2 medium zucchini, sliced
Grated Parmesan cheese

☐Brown sausage in a large pot. Drain off most of the fat and add onion and garlic; sauté, stirring, until limp. Stir in tomatoes, broth, wine, parsley, and basil. Simmer, uncovered, for 30 minutes. Add remaining ingredients and simmer, covered, until noodles are tender.

When served, pass around cheese. I prepare a day ahead and then add the noodles 20 to 30 minutes before serving.

Makes 8 servings.

Nancy Thompson
Portsmouth, Rhode Island

Dave's Note: Serve with warm, crusty bread, tossed salad, and whatever wine is left over from preparation. Makes a dandy meal for a group of hungry appetites.

BACON–CELERIAC SOUP

If you can't find any celeriac—don't make the soup.

6 strips bacon
1 medium onion, chopped
1¼ pounds celeriac,
 trimmed and sliced

2 medium potatoes, pared
 and sliced
1 medium carrot, pared
 and sliced

2½ cups chicken stock or
broth
¼ teaspoon dried
tarragon leaves
¼ teaspoon salt

¼ teaspoon freshly
ground white pepper
¾ to 1 cup milk or
half-and-half

☐ Sauté bacon over low heat until light brown and crisp. Remove bacon with slotted spoon and drain on paper toweling. Crumble into small pieces. Saute onion in bacon drippings until soft and light brown, about 5 minutes. Add celeriac, potatoes, and carrot to onion; stir in stock, tarragon, salt and pepper. Heat to boiling, then reduce heat and simmer, covered, until vegetables are tender, about 15 to 20 minutes.

Remove half of the vegetables with a slotted spoon to blender or food processor fitted with metal blade; purée, then transfer to a small bowl while you repeat with remaining vegetables. Add puréed vegetables to saucepan. Stir in milk to desired consistency and heat over very low heat until warm. Stir in bacon.

Serve right away to 6 hungry people.

Dave's

SAUERKRAUT SOUP
(*Lithuanian*)

3 pounds pork spareribs
3 quarts water
1 large onion, sliced
2 bay leaves
1 teaspoon salt

5 to 6 peppercorns
1 pound sauerkraut,
drained and rinsed
½ small head of cabbage,
cored and shredded

☐ Simmer ribs, partially covered, in the water with sliced onion, salt, bay leaves, and peppercorns for 1 hour. Add rinsed kraut; simmer for 30 minutes. Add cabbage and simmer 15 minutes longer. Ribs may be removed and served separately, or break the

meat into pieces and place in soup. Serve with rye bread or hot boiled potatoes.
Makes 12 servings.

Mrs. Mary A. Lukis
Walpole, Massachusetts

POLISH CABBAGE SOUP

3 pounds corned spareribs
1 quart sauerkraut
1 head cabbage, cored and shredded
2 slices salt pork, diced and fried

1 cup old-fashioned rolled oats
10 medium potatoes, cooked and mashed

☐Soak corned spareribs in water overnight. Drain. Cover with fresh water and parboil. Drain again and add fresh water and cook, partially covered, until tender. Put fresh cabbage and sauerkraut in a large pan; cover with water and parboil. Drain, add cooked spareribs with liquid (add more water if necessary) and fried salt pork. Cook, partially covered, until cabbage is done. About 10 to 15 minutes before the soup is done, add oatmeal. Just before serving, add mashed potatoes.
Makes 8 servings.

Mrs. Anna Curis
Millville, Massachusetts

ORIENTAL PORK CUCUMBER SOUP

This recipe was found on a torn scrap of newsprint, tucked into the pages of an old cookbook of my mother's. I don't remember her ever making it. However, it adapted so well to microwave cooking and is both economical and low in calories, so that it seems very much a "soup of today."

1 large green onion, thinly
    sliced
5 cups chicken broth (you
    can use broth packets)
2 tablespoons soy sauce
½ pound lean boneless
    pork, cut in thin strips

2 medium cucumbers,
    peeled, halved, seeded,
    and sliced ¼ inch thick
Green onion bits for
    garnish

☐In a microwave oven, cook onion in the broth and soy sauce
for 8 minutes. Add pork and cook for 2 minutes. Add cucumbers
and cook 7 minutes longer, until cucumbers are crisp-tender and
pork is tender.
    Makes 4 to 6 servings.

Phyllis W. McCarthy
Rutland, Massachusetts

NANA BEA'S CHICKEN SOUP

5 quarts water
1 whole onion, peeled
Salt and pepper to taste
2 chickens (3 pounds each),
    quartered
4 carrots, pared

4 stalks celery, trimmed
1 parsnip root, pared
2 stems fresh dill
5 to 6 stems fresh parsley
Cooked thin egg noodles

☐Fill a large pot with 5 quarts of water and add onion, salt, and
pepper and bring to a boil. Meanwhile, clean chickens well. Put
chickens into boiling water. When water comes to a boil again,
lower heat and simmer, partially covered, for 30 minutes. Skim
off fat and add carrots, celery, and parsnip. After 1 hour, add dill
and parsley tied together. Skim fat occasionally. Simmer slowly
for 1 hour longer.
    Remove chickens, carrots, and celery and set aside in a
bowl. Remove dill, parsley, parsnip, and onion and discard.
Then, with a sieve and cheesecloth, run soup through to remove

fat. Salt and pepper to taste.

Serve with very thin egg noodles, carrots and celery from soup, along with bits of chicken.

Makes 10 to 12 servings.

Mrs. Beatrice Susser
Little Silver, New Jersey

"MA BELLE'S" CHICKEN WING SOUP

As you probably know, Buffalo is famous for chicken wings and a lot of other good things. My dear mother believed that good natural food kept one healthy, hence Chicken Wing Soup. After the soup was cooked to Mom's taste, she would take out the wings, pick the meat off the bones, chop it up, and mix it with homemade salad dressing for sandwiches. My school lunches were the best. However, my husband, Ted, likes the cooked wings roasted in the oven, then he chews the meat from the bone. Any way you do it, it's delicious. Oh yes, you can take the meat off the bones and put it back in the soup.

8 chicken wings, rinsed
4 medium cloves garlic, cut up
1 large onion, chopped
2 medium carrots, pared and chopped
3 long stalks celery with leaves, chopped
3 chicken bouillon cubes
1 cup rice (white or brown)

☐Put rinsed chicken wings in a 6-quart kettle. Fill kettle with water, about 2 inches from top. Add remaining ingredients. Bring to a boil, skimming as necessary, then lower heat to simmer. Let simmer, partially covered, for about 3 hours. Add more water if needed.

When finished, chicken may be cut up into soup, or put in oven and covered with barbecue sauce. Terrific either way.

Makes 8 to 10 servings.

Mrs. Theodore R. Slifer
Buffalo, New York

CHICKEN SOUP WITH TORTILLA STRIPS

1 broiler-fryer chicken
(about 4 pounds)
7 cups water
3 small onions, cut into
quarters
3 medium tomatoes,
peeled and cut into
wedges
½ teaspoon crushed
dried hot red pepper

½ teaspoon ground
cumin
2 cups (1 pint) whipping
cream
Salt and pepper
½ cup fresh coriander
sprigs
Flour Tortilla Strips (recipe
follows)

☐Put the whole chicken, water, and onions in a 6- to 8-quart kettle. Cover and bring to a boil over high heat; reduce heat to medium and simmer, partially covered and skimming as necessary, until meat pulls easily from the bones, about 1 hour. Lift out chicken and cool. When cool enough to handle, pull meat in shreds from bones and set aside. Discard skin and bones. Boil broth, uncovered, to reduce to about 4 cups. Pour through a wire strainer and set broth aside.

Return cooked onions to kettle along with tomatoes, hot pepper, and cumin; stir over medium heat until tomatoes mash easily, about 10 minutes. Add reduced broth, cream, and chicken meat and return to a boil. Add salt and pepper to taste. Serve soup garnished with coriander and tortilla strips.

Makes 8 servings.

Flour Tortilla Strips

8 flour tortillas   1½ cups vegetable oil

☐To make tortilla strips, cut flour tortillas into 1-inch wide strips. Pour vegetable oil into a 10- to 12-inch frying pan over medium heat. Fry a few strips at a time, turning, until golden. Drain well on paper towels and serve warm. (Or store in an airtight container overnight. To rewarm, spread out on an ungreased baking sheet and set in a 350°F oven until hot.

Dave's

Dave's Note: Tortillas can be eaten out of hand or crumbled into soup.
Dave's Doublenote: A strawberry margarita beforehand would be a knock-out.

EASY CHICKEN SOUP ALMANDINE

1 medium onion, sliced
2 tablespoons safflower or
   peanut oil
3 cups chicken stock or
   broth
1 whole chicken breast,
   skinned, boned, and cut
   in half
3 tablespoons milk
2 slices day-old bread,
   crusts removed

¾ cup blanched almonds
1 egg yolk
1 tablespoon snipped fresh
   parsley, plus extra for
   garnish
½ teaspoon dried
   marjoram leaves
Salt and freshly ground
   pepper to taste

☐Preheat oven to 350°F.

Sauté onion in oil in medium saucepan over medium heat until soft and light brown, about 5 minutes. Stir in the stock, then add half of the chicken breast. Heat to boiling; reduce heat. Simmer, covered, until chicken is tender, about 5 to 10 minutes. Remove chicken with slotted spoon. Reserve chicken and liquid separately.

Spoon milk over bread in small bowl. Let stand until milk is absorbed. Place almonds in a food processor fitted with metal blade. Process until coarsely ground. Transfer to a small baking sheet. Bake in preheated oven, stirring occasionally, until light brown, about 5 minutes.

Place *uncooked* chicken (cut in cubes), the bread mixture, egg yolk, 1 tablespoon parsley, and ¼ teaspoon of the marjoram in food processor. Process until finely ground. Sprinkle with salt and pepper. Shape mixture into ½-inch balls.

Place nuts, remaining ¼ teaspoon marjoram and the cooked chicken (cubed) in food processor. Process until very finely ground. Stir into reserved broth. Heat over medium heat to simmering. Season to taste with salt and pepper. Stir chicken balls into broth; simmer gently until balls are tender and cooked through, approximately 15 to 20 minutes. Sprinkle with parsley. Dig in.

Makes 6 servings.

Dave's

CHINESE CHICKEN SOUP

1 small chicken
1 onion, chopped
1 stalk celery, trimmed, cut
  diagonally
½ green pepper, seeded
  and chopped (optional)
1 small can bean sprouts,
  undrained
1 can bamboo shoots,
  drained and sliced

1 can (3 ounces)
  mushrooms, drained
1 can (5 ounces) water
  chestnuts, drained and
  sliced
1 teaspoon soy sauce
Pepper
1 small tomato, seeded

☐ Boil chicken in salted water until tender. Save broth and cut up chicken meat. Reserve. Add onion, celery, and green pepper to broth. Simmer for 15 minutes. Add undrained bean sprouts, bamboo shoots, mushrooms, water chestnuts, soy sauce, and salt and pepper to taste. Add chicken to broth and heat through. Just before serving, add tomato for color.

Makes 8 servings.

Flo Maine
North Reading, Massachusetts

MULLIGATAWNY SOUP

1 roasting chicken (4 to 5
    pounds), cut up
⅓ cup unsifted
    all-purpose flour
⅓ cup butter
1½ cups chopped onion
2 cups chopped pared
    carrot
2 cups chopped celery
1½ cups chopped pared
    apple
1½ tablespoons curry
    powder

4 teaspoons salt
¾ teaspoon ground mace
Pepper to taste
¼ teaspoon chili powder
¾ cup flaked coconut
6 cups cold water
1 cup light cream
1 cup apple juice
1½ cups hot, cooked rice
½ cup chopped fresh
    parsley

☐Wash chicken and pat dry. Roll in flour; reserve remaining flour. Sauté chicken in butter in large kettle or Dutch oven until well browned on all sides. Remove chicken from kettle and set aside. Add onion, carrot, celery, apple, and remaining flour to kettle. Cook, stirring, for 5 minutes. Add curry powder, salt, mace, pepper, chili powder, coconut, and the cold water; mix well. Add chicken, turning to cook. Bring to a boil and reduce heat. Cover and simmer for 2 hours, stirring occasionally.

Remove pot from heat. Skim fat from soup. Remove chicken pieces and discard skin and bones. Cut chicken into small pieces. Return meat to kettle, with apple juice and light cream. Reheat.

To serve, place a heaping spoonful of rice in each of 6 bowls. Add soup and sprinkle with parsley.

Makes 6 servings.

Barbara Sessewicz
Norwell, Massachusetts

Dave's Note: It's sort of a kitchen sink recipe, with a lot of latitude for the cook. Nice, snappy flavor either way.

FRENCHMAN'S SOUP

This soup started with my husband's grandmother, who was originally from Canada. She called it "red soup," but somehow through the years it has become known as "Frenchman's soup." Her stock was derived from leftover pork or beef roasts or turkey bones simmered with spices, chopped onions, and celery. I also do this when I have a roast or turkey, but I like my soup stock best from chicken.

3 pounds chicken wings
1 cup water
1 large onion, chopped
2 stalks celery with leaves,
    chopped
Salt and pepper to taste

4 chicken bouillon cubes
4 cups boiling water
2 cans (16 ounces each)
    stewed tomatoes
1 cup assorted pasta

☐ Pressure-cook chicken wings, water, onion, celery, and salt and pepper to taste for 20 minutes at 10 pounds pressure. Cool for 5 minutes and release pressure gradually. Remove chicken wings from stock. Discard bones and skin, cut chicken into small pieces. Refrigerate stock overnight, or until fat rises to top and hardens. Lift off with a spoon and discard. (If you do not have a pressure cooker, simmer ingredients, covered, for 1½ hours on your stove).

Dissolve bouillon cubes in 4 cups boiling water. Purée tomatoes in blender. Using an 8-quart pot, combine the two chicken broths, tomatoes, and salt and pepper. Bring to a boil and add assorted pasta. (I use a combination of soup macs, elbow macaroni, broken noodles, broken pieces of spaghetti, etc.—anything you have on hand.) Reduce heat and simmer for 10 to 12 minutes. Add cubed chicken and serve with hot rolls and a salad for a complete meal.

Makes 8 servings.

C. Jean Trottier
Hollis, New Hampshire

GRANDMA ROSE'S FOWL AND BEEF SOUP

This recipe has been in my present family since I was married 42½ years ago. My mother-in-law made it all her grown-up life, and the Lord knows how long it was in her parents' and grandparents' lives. So we call it "Grandma Rose's soup." Grandma Rose was Italian! I make it whenever I can find a fowl or, as it is also called, a stewing hen. The fall is the best time to buy a fowl, and it pays to pick up a few for the freezer. Although Grandma Rose used to serve it like a boiled dinner is served, I am lazy and serve it with all the meat cut up into pieces and returned to the pot. I add the vermicelli to the amount of soup I plan to use at a particular meal.

1 fowl	Potatoes
Shank bone with meat on it	Carrots
(1 or 2 pounds)	Onions
1 can (16 ounces) tomatoes	Salt and pepper to taste
Parsley	Vermicelli
A couple of bay leaves	Grated Parmesan cheese

☐Simmer fowl and beef shank in enough water to cover with tomatoes, bay leaf, and parsley for about 2½ hours. Add potatoes, carrots, and onions (cut vegetables into size you prefer) along with salt and pepper to taste. Cook about 30 minutes, or until vegetables are done. Remove fowl, meat, and vegetables and serve as a boiled dinner, after serving the soup with curled vermicelli in it and sprinkled with Parmesan cheese.

Mrs. Stephen Donahue
Shrewsbury, Massachusetts

KENTUCKY BURGOO

Burgoo was made famous by Irvin Cobb and served at auctions, fairs, homecomings, etc.

2 pounds pork shanks
1 pound veal shanks
2 pounds breast of lamb
1 chicken (4 to 6 pounds)
1 rabbit (optional)
1 squirrel (optional)
2 pounds potatoes, pared
  and diced
2 pounds onions, diced
1 bunch carrots, pared and
  chopped
3 green peppers, seeded
  and chopped
2 cups chopped cabbage

4 cups tomato purée
3 cups fresh or canned
  corn kernels
2 pods red pepper
2 cups sliced okra
2 cups lima beans
1 cup diced celery
Salt and cayenne pepper to
  taste
Chopped fresh parsley
Tabasco sauce
A-1 sauce
Worcestershire sauce

☐Put the meats in cold water and bring to a boil, skimming as necessary. Reduce heat and stew slowly till meat falls from the bones. Remove meat to cool and chop; discard bones. Prepare vegetables and return with meat and remaining ingredients to the stock and simmer until very thick. It can not overcook if you keep stirring it (with a wooden spoon) and do not let it stick down.
Makes 20 to 25 servings.

Pauline Nazor
Concord, Massachusetts

CREOLE GUMBO

½ pound uncooked ham,
  preferably country style
1 chicken, cut up
All-purpose flour for
  dredging chicken
2 cups fresh or 1 package
  (10 ounces) frozen okra,
  thawed if frozen
2 onions, minced
Butter

1 small hot red pepper
1 can (16 ounces) tomatoes
3 quarts boiling water
1 bay leaf
1 teaspoon gumbo filé
Salt and pepper to taste
Oysters or crabmeat or
  both
Hot, cooked rice

☐Fry ham, dice, and set aside. Dredge chicken in flour and sauté well on all sides in ham fat. Remove chicken, dice meat, and set aside. Add okra and minced onion to skillet. Cook, stirring occasionally, for about 10 minutes. Add butter if needed. Pour mixture into a large pot and add red pepper, diced chicken, diced ham, tomatoes, boiling water, and bay leaf. Simmer very slowly for 2 hours. Season with gumbo filé. Just before serving, add oysters and/or crab and heat through. Serve on a bed of rice. Makes 8 to 10 servings.

Pauline Nazor
Concord, Massachusetts

FISH STOCK FOR SOUP OR CHOWDER

This is my basic recipe for fish stock. I've varied the herbs from time to time, but I pretty much always come back to this.

Gutted fish with fillets removed
Clam, shrimp, or lobster shells
2½ cups cold water
½ cup chopped onion
½ cup chopped celery with leaves
6 peppercorns

4 cloves
A little lemon rind
1 carrot
2 sprigs fresh thyme
2 sprigs fresh parsley
½ to 1 cup dry white wine
1 bay leaf

☐Chop up remaining parts of fish (don't use strong-flavored fish like mackerel) into large pieces. Remove and discard gills—everything else goes into the pot. Put in leftover shells. Put all of the remaining ingredients into the pot and bring to a boil. Simmer, uncovered, for 15 minutes. (Overcooking makes it taste bitter, so keep taste-testing it to make sure you're not overcooking.) Remove from the heat, skim, and strain it. Refrigerate if not ready to use right away.

Makes about 3 cups.

Remember chowder should be allowed to ripen overnight in the refrigerator. Add fish chunks 8 to 10 minutes before serving.

Dave's

CREOLE BISQUE

Cooking is almost therapeutic; it's the best way I've found to relax. Eating is one of the basic human joys. I had a family of ten children to practice on. This recipe is dietetic, too—only 161 calories per 1-cup serving.

2 tablespoons butter
2 tablespoons all-purpose flour
1½ teaspoons seasoned salt
1 can (16 ounces) stewed tomatoes with onion and pepper

½ pound sole or haddock fillets, cut in 1-inch pieces
½ pound zucchini, scrubbed and sliced ¼ inch thick
2 cups milk

☐Melt butter in a heavy 2-quart saucepan over low heat. Stir in flour and salt until mixture is smooth. Stir in tomatoes and add fish and zucchini. Bring to a boil; reduce heat, then cover and simmer for 5 to 10 minutes or until fish is opaque and zucchini is tender. Stir in milk. Heat to serving temperature.

Makes 5½ cups.

Yvette Laprode
Spencer, Massachusetts

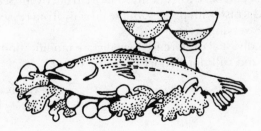

EASY FISH CHOWDER

I'm sure that I could build a heck of a background story for this recipe by saying that it came from my wife's great uncle who was a sea captain or even through my ancestors, Loyalists who were driven to Nova Scotia with the British during the evacuation of Boston. But, in truth, I originally found the basis upon which I built this recipe in a trade-type commercial fishing publication about four or five years ago. I think the unique thing about the recipe is that I have never made it the same way twice. If one really likes a good fish chowder, I believe this will match the best anywhere, and it is *very* easy to prepare.

2 pounds haddock or cod
  fillets
3 medium onions, sliced
1 bay leaf
½ cup butter
1 garlic clove, chopped or
  pressed
2 teaspoons chili powder
  (optional)
½ cup rosé wine
  (optional)
4 potatoes, pared and
  sliced
2½ teaspoons salt

½ cup chopped celery
  leaves
¼ teaspoon ground
  white pepper
¼ teaspoon cayenne
  pepper (optional)
¼ teaspoon dill seed
  (optional)
2 cups boiling water
2 cups light sweet cream or
  milk
2 sprigs fresh parsley,
  chopped

☐ Preheat oven to 375°F. Put all the ingredients except the sweet cream and parsley into a 3-quart casserole dish (place fillets on top). Cover and bake for 1 hour. Remove from oven. Scald cream and add. Garnish with parsley. Serve directly from casserole dish.
  Makes 8 servings.
  Note: Individual preference may dictate modification of spices and wine and will not detract from the recipe.

David Goldthwaite
Hudson, New Hampshire

CLAM CHOWDER

2 cans (7½ ounces each)
    chopped clams
1½ cups clam juice
½ cup water
3 potatoes, pared and diced
1 teaspoon salt
1 large or 2 small bay
    leaves
½ teaspoon pepper

1 tablespoon
    Worcestershire sauce
6 ounces salt pork, finely
    diced
1 cup diced onion
3½ tablespoons all-purpose
    flour
1 cup milk
½ cup light cream

☐Heat clams, clam juice, water, potatoes, and seasonings in a pan. In another pan, render the salt pork and sauté the onion until transparent. Add the flour and cook for about 10 minutes, stirring constantly. Add to liquid mixture and thicken with milk and cream.
Makes 4 servings.

C. M. Anderson
Worcester, Massachusetts

FRESH SHRIMP CHOWDER

Prepare this chowder several hours before serving; let set.

1 large onion, chopped
2 tablespoons butter
1 large carrot, pared and
    diced
1½ cups diced pared
    potatoes
3 tablespoons all-purpose
    flour
1 cup (approximately)
    chicken stock

⅛ teaspoon seasoned salt
Black pepper to taste
Paprika to taste
1½ cups milk
2 cups shrimp, peeled and
    deveined
Chopped fresh parsley

☐Sauté onion in butter and add carrot and diced potatoes. Cover with water and simmer, covered, on low heat until the vegetables are tender. In a small bowl, mix the flour and some of the soup liquid to make a paste. Add more soup liquid and then return all to the pot. Add stock, seasoned salt, pepper, paprika, and milk. Turn off heat.

Sauté the shrimp in butter, turning once in frying pan. Add shrimp to the pot, cover, and let set for several hours.

At dinner time, heat through and sprinkle a little parsley in the pot and stir. Serve at once.

Makes 8 servings.

Hilda and Bill Berry
Nobleboro, Maine

CAPE BRETON FISH CHOWDER

I was introduced to this chowder while visiting relatives in Sydney, Cape Breton, although the recipe comes from Glace Bay, Cape Breton. When this chowder is made there it is usually tripled, resulting in a big pot that is left on the stove for anyone to help themselves to. Since the Cape Bretoners are a friendly lot, their home is always open to family, friends, and friends of friends, so if anyone knows that a pot is being made, they always drop in and help themselves to a bowl. First thing you know, there's an empty pot. Although I do not know how old this recipe is, it is the best chowder I have ever tasted.

¼ to ½ pound butter
1 onion, diced
Salt and pepper to taste
Cayenne pepper to taste
1 pound mixed fish (any white fish, scallops, and shrimp)
1 cup diced pared carrot

1 can (3 ounces) mushrooms
1 tablespoon processed cheese spread
Paprika to taste
Parsley flakes
2 cups diced pared potatoes

1 can (10½ ounces) cream
of celery soup
1 can (10½ ounces) cream
of mushroom soup
1 quart milk

1 tablespoon prepared
mustard
1 can (7½ ounces) chopped
clams

☐Melt butter in a large saucepan and sauté onion; add salt, pepper, and cayenne to taste, along with fresh fish, scallops, and shrimp. Cook until soft and add remaining ingredients. Simmer until vegetables are tender. For an extra touch of elegance, add lobster.

Makes 8 servings.

Lorraine Hullu
Plainstow, New Hampshire

MACDOUGAL'S BAKED FISH CHOWDER

It may have started back in Oban, Scotland. There is a MacDougal (my maiden name) castle there. I came to Kittery after I was married and had a seafood restaurant there for a long time. I am not skilled at thinking up fancy names. This dish has always been called "baked fish chowder," and all I can think of to be different would be to put the MacDougal name on it and call it "MacDougal's baked fish chowder."

2 pounds haddock fillets
1 or 2 small onions, finely
chopped
4 potatoes, pared and finely
cut
½ cup butter or
margarine
2½ teaspoons salt

½ teaspoon dried dill
1 small clove garlic,
chopped or pressed
1 ounce dry vermouth or
white wine
2 cups boiling water
2 cups light cream

☐Preheat oven to 375°F.

Put all the ingredients except the cream into a large, deep casserole dish. Cover and bake for 1 hour. Remove from oven and stir in cream.

Makes 8 servings.

Mrs. Roger Freeman
Kittery, Maine

LEAH'S FISH CHOWDER

This recipe originated here in Cushing, Maine, with my grandmother, Leah Payson, and is the best fish chowder I've ever had. Hope you agree.

¼ pound salt pork, sliced
2 onions, finely chopped
2 pounds haddock fillets
3 to 4 cups diced pared
   potatoes
1 quart milk, scalded
1 can (13 ounces)
   evaporated milk
½ cup butter
Salt and pepper to taste

☐Fry salt pork in a heavy pot until completely melted. Remove rind and discard. Cook onions in fat until clear. Meanwhile, place haddock fillets in a cheesecloth bag and cook in boiling water until just tender, about 10 minutes. Remove bag, and in the same water cook potatoes until tender, about 5 minutes. Drain potatoes. Flake fish and add to cooked onions. Then add cooked potatoes, scalded milk, evaporated milk, butter, and seasonings. Place on the back of your wood stove or on *warm* burner until ready to serve. Serve with old-fashioned soda crackers.

Makes 8 servings.

June Kinne
Cushing, Maine

FISH CHOWDER

This fish chowder recipe has been handed down to me by my mother and to her by her mother. I have had a restaurant owner ask to try the recipe, and I have made it many times, and it has never failed to bring great responses from everyone who enjoys it.

2 pounds haddock or cod	½ teaspoon pepper
2 cans (11½ ounces each) chopped clams, drained but liquid reserved	1½ teaspoons sugar
	⅛ teaspoon dried thyme
	⅛ teaspoon cayenne pepper
¼ pound salt pork	4 tablespoons butter
4 medium onions, sliced	½ cup all-purpose flour
4 medium potatoes, pared and cubed	1 quart whole milk
2 teaspoons salt	1 cup light cream

☐Cut fish into large chunks and place in a saucepan. Add water to cover and cook, uncovered, over low heat for about 15 minutes, until fish is tender. Remove fish and cool. Strain liquid and set aside. Cut clams in pieces and reserve liquid. Cut salt pork in small pieces and fry in a skillet until crisp. Remove salt pork and discard. Add onions to fat in pan and sauté for about 10 minutes. Add potatoes, salt, pepper, sugar, thyme, cayenne, fish and clam liquids, and enough water to cover potatoes. Cover tightly and cook until potatoes are tender. Add fish and clams. In a separate pan, melt butter and add flour, stirring constantly over low heat. Add milk gradually and continue to stir constantly until thickened. Stir in cream and add the white sauce to the fish chowder. Simmer over low heat for 15 minutes.

Mrs. John Powers
Swansea, Massachusetts

NEW ORLEANS CHOWDER

1 teaspoon chopped onion
1 small clove garlic,
   minced
1 tablespoon butter or
   margarine

1 can (10½ ounces)
   Campbell's Chicken
   Gumbo Soup
1 soup can water
½ cup flaked, cooked fish

☐In a saucepan, cook onion and garlic in butter until tender. Add remaining ingredients. Heat through, stirring occasionally. Makes 2 to 3 servings.

Frances and S. Muzzy Perla
Leominster, Massachusetts

SALMON CHOWDER

¼ pound salt pork,
   cubed
6 small potatoes, pared and
   diced
2 onions, finely chopped
3 cups boiling water
1 can (15½ ounces) red
   salmon, undrained

2 cups milk
1 tablespoon all-purpose
   flour
Salt and pepper to taste
1 tablespoon minced fresh
   parsley

☐Fry salt pork in a deep kettle; when crisp, remove pieces of pork and put potatoes and onions in kettle. Cover with boiling water. Simmer, covered, over low heat for 30 minutes, or until potatoes are tender. Add salmon with liquid (remove small bones), milk, and flour; cook for 5 minutes longer. Season with salt and pepper. Add minced parsley before serving. Makes 6 servings.

Mrs. Florence Fitzgerald
Lynn, Massachusetts

SICILIAN FISH SOUP

1 cup coarsely chopped
   onion
½ cup chopped green
   pepper
3 cloves garlic, crushed
½ cup olive oil
1 can (28 ounces) Italian
   plum tomatoes
1 cup water
½ cup dry white wine
2 cups diced pared
   potatoes
2 teaspoons salt

1 teaspoon fennel seed
¼ teaspoon freshly
   ground pepper
2 pounds haddock fillets,
   fresh or frozen, cut in
   2-inch-wide pieces
½ teaspoon dried
   oregano
½ teaspoon dried basil
½ teaspoon dried thyme
7 tablespoons grated
   Parmesan cheese

☐ Sauté onions, green pepper, and garlic in hot oil in a large saucepan until onions are tender. Add tomatoes, water, wine, potatoes, salt, fennel seed, and pepper. Bring to a boil, then reduce heat, cover, and simmer for 30 minutes. Add haddock, oregano, basil, and thyme; cook for 10 minutes, or until fish flakes easily when tested with fork. Ladle into warm soup plates. Sprinkle each serving with 1 tablespoon Parmesan cheese. Serve immediately.

Makes 8 servings.

Dave's

G.G.'S LOBSTER BISQUE

This lobster bisque was my mother's and was always the crowning glory of a lobster feed.

1 boiled lobster, shells and
   meat
3½ cups water
1 tablespoon butter

½ medium green pepper,
   seeded and finely
   chopped
1 stalk celery, finely chopped

1 medium onion, finely
  chopped
1 cup water
1 tablespoon all-purpose
  flour

½ can (13 ounces)
  evaporated milk
Salt and pepper to taste

☐Pick meat from lobster shells and set aside. Crush shells, then place in a kettle with 2½ cups of the water. Cook gently, uncovered, for 10 minutes or until about 2 cups of liquid is left. Strain liquid, discarding shells, and reserve.

In a skillet, cook pepper, celery, and onion, uncovered, in butter and remaining 1 cup water until water has evaporated and vegetables are cooked. Add flour and mix thoroughly; add reserved lobster stock slowly, stirring constantly. Add evaporated milk. Strain out pepper, celery, and onion and discard. Add lobster meat to bisque and season as desired.

Makes 6 servings.

Charlotte Grant
Concord, New Hampshire

OYSTER BISQUE

1 quart shelled oysters,
  undrained
3 tablespoons butter
3 tablespoons all-purpose
  flour
2 cups milk
1 cup light cream

Salt
1 tablespoon
  Worcestershire sauce
¼ cup heavy cream
2 tablespoons diced
  pimiento

☐Inspect oysters carefully. Place 1 tablespoon of the butter in skillet; add oysters and cook them in their own liquor until the edges curl. Force oysters through a coarse sieve and mix with liquor.

In a separate saucepan, melt remaining 2 tablespoons butter over low heat. Gradually stir in flour until smooth. Add milk and light cream, stirring constantly until thickened. Season with ½ teaspoon salt and the Worcestershire sauce. Combine with oyster purée just before serving. Garnish with pimiento cream, made by mixing heavy cream, salt, and pimiento rubbed through a sieve, then beating until stiff.

Makes 6 servings.

Dave's

Dave's Note: Very good. I like the pimiento cream garnish.

CLAM AND MUSHROOM SOUP

3 cups chicken stock
1 cup chopped fresh
**   mushrooms**
2 shallots, minced
1 can (15 ounces) New
**   England–style clam**
**   chowder**

1 cup milk
¼ cup sour cream
Salt and freshly ground
**   pepper**
Fresh parsley sprigs

☐Bring chicken stock to boil in medium saucepan. Add mushrooms and shallots. Reduce heat and simmer, uncovered, for 10 minutes. Blend in chowder, milk, and sour cream and heat through; do not boil. Season with salt and pepper. Ladle into bowls and garnish with parsley.

Makes 4 to 6 servings.

Dave's

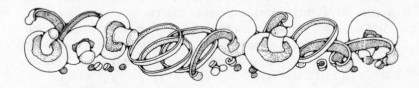

VAGABOND VEGETABLE SOUP

Winters used to be much colder and snowier way back then, and I can remember parking my sled and coming into my grandmother's warm kitchen for a bowl of this hearty soup—pure heaven! Over the years, my mother added her touch, and now, with the new products in the markets, I have added even more. I think it's appropriate to say "just put in everything but the kitchen sink"! The secret, of course, is the rich broth you're starting with.

1 handful dried white beans
1 handful dried chick-peas
1 handful barley
Shin beef (about 2 pounds)
1 whole chicken (2 to 3 pounds)
1 bay leaf
1 can of soup starter or 1 package dry mix
1 medium turnip, pared and diced

3 carrots, pared and sliced
2 stalks celery, chopped
4 medium onions, sliced
3 medium parsnips, pared and sliced
1 can (16 ounces) crushed tomatoes
1 package (16 ounces) frozen mixed vegetables
Salt and pepper to taste

☐ The night before, soak white beans, chick-peas and barley in water. In a large pot, brown a nice, solid meaty piece of shin beef. Add whole chicken, bay leaf, soup starter, beans, and barley, salt to taste, and cover with water. Bring to a boil, skimming as necessary, then reduce heat and simmer gently, partially covered, about 1 hour. Remove chicken when tender. Add diced turnip, carrots, celery, onions, and parsnips. Simmer soup until beef is done, about 1 hour longer. Remove beef and cut into small pieces. Skin chicken; remove bones and cut up meat into pieces. Add beef and chicken meat to soup. Add crushed tomatoes and mixed vegetables. Simmer for 5 to 10 minutes more and taste for seasoning. Continue to simmer for approximately 1½ to 2 hours. Make 10 to 12 servings.

Ruth Jewell
Rockport, Massachusetts

SOUP AS A MEAL

1 large sweet potato or 2
  small, pared and cubed
1½ pounds or more of
  butternut or any winter
  squash or pumpkin,
  pared and cubed
1 large onion, chopped
2 chicken bouillon cubes
½ cup chopped celery

1 teaspoon butter
1 cup or more of water
1 can (16 ounces) red
  kidney beans, drained
Bread slices
Salt and pepper to taste
Vinegar to taste
Fresh mint sprigs

☐Mix the first eight ingredients in a large saucepan. Simmer, covered, until all the ingredients are cooked. I like to sauté the onions before adding them to the soup. Toast slices of bread and put one slice in each soup bowl. Pour soup over the bread and add salt, pepper, and vinegar. Add a sprig of mint. Serve with a salad.
  Makes 8 servings.

Anna Gallagher
Fall River, Massachusetts

MINESTRONE SOUP
(Appetizer)

¼ pound string beans,
  cut in ½-inch pieces
½ pound peas, shelled
3 stalks celery, finely
  chopped
1 large potato, pared and
  finely diced
2 carrots, pared and finely
  chopped
1 small turnip, pared and
  finely diced

3 tablespoons olive oil
Salt and pepper to taste
1 tablespoon chopped fresh
  parsley
1 clove garlic, minced
1 can (16 ounces) plum
  tomatoes, mashed
2 pounds escarole, cut up
½ teaspoon dried
  oregano
2 quarts water

1 can (19 ounces) white cannellini beans, undrained	1 can (19 ounces) chick-peas, undrained
1 can (19 ounces) red kidney beans, undrained	

☐In a 5-quart pot, toss string beans, peas, celery, potato, carrots, turnip, and garlic with oil. Cook, covered, on medium heat for 10 minutes, or until vegetables are slightly soft. Add salt and pepper to taste with parsley, tomatoes, escarole, oregano, and 2 quarts of water. Bring to boil, cover, and cook on medium-low heat until escarole is cooked, about 20 minutes. Add the beans and cook on medium-low heat for 15 minutes longer.

Makes 12 servings.

Christine Quinn
Sterling, Massachusetts

HEARTY VEGETABLE-RICE SOUP

This old family recipe offers a great versatile appeal because it presents the opportunity to improvise in the utilization of assorted vegetables that offer both appealing taste and nutritious eating; fresh-cut corn or lima beans are also very good in it. A great "warmer up" for a cold day.

3 quarts water (approximately)	1 cup shredded cabbage
1 pound beef short ribs	2 tomatoes, chopped
2 cloves garlic, minced	¼ cup red wine
2 medium onions, chopped	1 can (6 ounces) tomato paste
1 cup diced celery	¼ cup sugar
1 cup diced pared carrot	1 cup rice
1 tablespoon chopped fresh parsley	Seasoning to taste (salt, pepper, basil)
1 bouillon cube dissolved in 1 cup water	

☐Combine water, meat, garlic, and onions in a large pot. Cover and cook until meat is tender. Skim any fat off the top. Add the remaining ingredients, except rice, cover, and cook for about 3 hours over low heat. (More water may be added if soup becomes too thick.) Add rice, cover, and cook for another 45 minutes to an hour and serve.
Makes 8 to 10 servings.

Betty Schartl
Mansfield, Ohio

VEGETABLE CHOWDER

6 large potatoes, pared and cubed
5 to 6 onions, chopped
4 stalks celery, cut in ½-inch pieces
1 green pepper, seeded and chopped
1 cup chopped salted peanuts
1 can (10½ ounces) condensed tomato soup
1 can (16 ounces) cream-style corn

2 soup cans of milk
1 package (10 ounces) frozen green beans
½ teaspoon dried basil
1 teaspoon minced fresh parsley
½ teaspoon dried marjoram or 1½ teaspoons chopped fresh
1 can (10½ ounces) green pea soup
Salt to taste

☐Mix everything together in a large heavy saucepan. Bring to a boil and reduce heat; cook slowly, covered, until potatoes and celery are tender, about 20 minutes.
Makes 8 servings.

Eleanor McLear
Swansea, Massachusetts

VEGETABLE SOUP

My daughters (four) and my grandchildren (nine) all love this soup. I'm sorry it doesn't have a special name. An elderly person passed this recipe on to me many years ago when I started to have my grandchildren. She called it "kiddies' vegetable soup." Some of my friends to whom I have given this recipe use Vegall instead of the frozen vegetables. I wouldn't use anything but chopped sirloin. I figure it's good to use the best all the way.

1 pound ground beef
2 quarts chicken stock
1 quart water
1 envelope onion soup mix
2 stalks celery, thinly sliced

1 can (16 ounces) tomatoes, finely chopped
1 package (10 ounces) frozen vegetables
½ cup orzo pasta

☐ Brown beef in a large saucepan, then add chicken stock, water, and soup mix and boil for 20 minutes. Add vegetables and orzo. Boil for an additional 15 minutes.

Makes about 3 quarts.

Evelyn M. Croteau
Attleboro, Massachusetts

IRISH CABBAGE SOUP

If I had kissed the Blarney Stone, I could say that my dear old grandmother brought this recipe from the old country—however, my dear friend Rita gave it to me (she'll be furious when she sees this in print—probably obtained it the same way. However, she listens to the wrong radio station anyway) and it is a family favorite. Delicious!

3 tablespoons chopped onion	¾ teaspoon salt
3 tablespoons margarine	½ teaspoon nutmeg
¼ cup pared and chopped potatoes	1 tablespoon all-purpose flour
3 cups finely chopped cabbage	2 cups broth or water
	2½ cups milk
	Chopped fresh parsley

☐Sauté onion in margarine until tender. Add all the other ingredients except the milk and parsley and cook for 20 minutes. Purée in blender, add milk, and reheat. Can be served hot or cold. Garnish with chopped parsley.
Makes 5 cups.

Nancy E. Dunn
Pomfret Center, Connecticut

GREEN SOUP

This recipe was given to me by a very dear friend over forty years ago. She served it with her marvelous Irish bread! I never could duplicate her Irish bread. She kept a cow and churned her own butter. It was the buttermilk with the little pieces of golden butter floating in it that made all the difference. She used currants or raisins in it and baked it in a round pan. This is quickly made, healthful, and delicious.

½ medium head green cabbage, cored and cut up	1 medium onion, quartered
2 large stalks green celery, chopped	1½ cups water
	4 sprigs fresh parsley
1 large potato, pared and quartered	1 cup light cream or evaporated milk
	1 teaspoon salt
	¼ teaspoon black pepper

☐Cook cabbage, celery, potato, and onion in the water, covered, until tender. Put in blender and run on high speed for 1½ minutes. Add remaining ingredients and run on low speed for 15 seconds until mixed. Reheat to serve. Do not boil.
Makes 4 to 6 servings.

Kay Slattery
Scarborough, Maine

RUSSIAN CABBAGE SOUP

3 cups chicken broth
3 cups water
¼ cup shredded pared
    carrots
½ cup chopped celery
1 potato, pared and diced
½ cup chopped onion
2 cups chopped, peeled
    fresh tomatoes

2½ teaspoons salt
1 bay leaf
4 whole peppercorns
3 cups shredded cabbage
¼ cup fresh lemon juice
1 tablespoon sugar

☐Combine all the ingredients except the cabbage, lemon juice, and sugar in a large kettle. Bring to a boil, then reduce heat and simmer, covered, for 1 hour, stirring occasionally. Add cabbage and simmer for 10 minutes longer. Stir in lemon juice and sugar; heat.
Makes 6 to 8 servings.

Mrs. Florence Maria Galvin
Chelsea, Massachusetts

RAVIOLI AND CABBAGE SOUP

¼ pound bacon
1 small onion, chopped
2 cloves garlic, pressed or
    minced

1 tablespoon chopped fresh
    parsley
2 quarts beef broth
2 cups water

2 cups shredded cabbage   1 pound fresh or frozen
1 large carrot, pared and   ravioli
   thinly sliced   Grated Parmesan cheese

☐Cut bacon into ½-inch sections. In a 5- to 6-quart saucepan, stir bacon over medium heat until translucent. Add onion, garlic, and parsley. Continue stirring until onion and bacon are lightly browned. Add broth, water, cabbage, and carrot. Bring to a boil over high heat. Separate ravioli, if connected, and add to the boiling soup. Boil gently, uncovered, over medium heat, stirring occasionally, until ravioli are tender to bite, about 10 minutes for fresh ravioli, 12 minutes for frozen.
Ladle soup into bowls. Sprinkle grated Parmesan cheese over individual servings.
Makes 4 to 6 servings.

Dave's

SAUERKRAUT SOUP
(Kapusniak)

1 can (16½ ounces)   2 cloves garlic, chopped
   sauerkraut, drained and   1 can (12 ounces) beer
   rinsed   2 slices of salt pork, diced
1 can (10½ ounces)   Pepper to taste
   undiluted chicken soup   Kielbasa or hot dogs, sliced

☐Mix all ingredients except kielbasa in a large saucepan. Simmer, covered, for an hour, and during the last 10 minutes add sliced kielbasa or hot dogs.
Makes 8 servings.

Mrs. R. E. Hickman
Arnold, Maryland

LITHUANIAN LAPENI

This is an old Lithuanian spinach soup made by my mother. I have been making it for fifty-two years and have passed it on to my family and grandchildren. It's a great soup, and everyone who has tried it has liked it. Ham pieces can be used instead of bacon.

2 quarts water	1 large onion, diced
½ to ¾ cup barley	4 medium potatoes
½ pound bacon, diced	1 pound fresh spinach

☐Bring water to a boil and add barley; simmer, covered, for 1 hour. Meanwhile, fry bacon until crisp and drain on paper towels. Cook onion in bacon fat until transparent but not brown and remove from fat. Add bacon and onion to barley water. Peel potatoes and cut into cubes; add to soup. Clean spinach and remove stems; add leaves to soup. Season to taste and let simmer, covered, until potatoes and spinach are tender, about 20 minutes.
    Makes 8 servings.

Mildred E. Moreau
Worcester, Massachusetts

PROVINCETOWN KALE SOUP

My introduction to Provincetown kale soup occurred on a date. I had dinner at the Race Point Coast Guard Station. A female dining there with a room full of seafaring men was very rare. The chief cook served kale soup, a big favorite of the P-town Portuguese. I had never had it, and it surely hit the spot. Kale is popular around these parts now, and when I make this soup that memorable dinner flashes in my mind—the station overlooking the dunes and ocean with all of those wonderful local Coast Guardsmen. Sweet memories.

1 pound pea beans
2 pounds kale, broken in
pieces
½ pound linquica or
chorico (Portuguese
sausage), cut up

1 large onion, sliced
1 tablespoon vinegar
Salt and freshly ground
pepper to taste
11 cups water
6 small potatoes, pared

☐ Soak beans overnight in cold water. In the morning, drain and add kale, sausage, onion, vinegar, salt, and pepper with 10 cups of the water. Bring to a boil, then reduce heat and cook gently, covered, for 2 to 3 hours. Add potatoes and remaining 1 cup water. Continue cooking until potatoes are tender, about 30 minutes. Eat with a chunk of fresh bread and cheese.
   Makes 8 servings.

Gloria Donnelly
West Boylston, Massachusetts

BECK'S HEARTY BEAN SOUP

This recipe was a joint effort, concocted by my late husband and myself about forty years ago. We combined a bit of his Midwest Dutch with my New England touch, and came up with a sturdy soup that hit the spot. A little imagination goes a long way when trying to make ends meet.

1½ to 2 cups dried navy
beans
1 meaty ham bone or 2
smoked ham hocks
1 whole onion
3 to 3½ quarts water
1 cup finely chopped,
pared carrot
½ cup finely chopped
celery

½ cup finely chopped
onion
1 teaspoon salt
¼ teaspoon pepper
Vinegar
Cooked noodles (optional)
Light cream or milk
(optional)
Ground cinnamon
(optional)

☐Pick over beans and soak in water overnight. Drain and add 3 to 3½ quarts water, ham bone, and whole onion. Cover and simmer for about 3 hours until beans are tender, adding more water if necessary. Remove and discard onion, bone, and fat. Finely chop any ham and return to pot. Add carrot, celery, chopped onion, salt, and pepper. Simmer, covered, for about 1 hour.

When served, add a dash of vinegar and more salt and pepper if needed.

To make it more interesting, add cooked noodles to pot when vegetables are done, and simmer for 5 to 10 minutes. For a cream soup, add the noodles plus light cream or milk to the pot and simmer for a few minutes, about 5 to 10 minutes. Add the vinegar to each bowl and a dash of cinnamon.

Makes 10 to 12 servings.

Rita Weissbeck
Lowell, Massachusetts

SENATE BEAN SOUP

1 pound dried navy or
    Great Northern beans
5 quarts water
1 smoked ham bone
1 cup chopped celery

3 potatoes, cooked and
    mashed
1 cup chopped onion
2 cloves garlic, minced
Salt and pepper to taste

☐Wash beans and soak overnight in a large kettle. Drain and add 5 quarts water and ham bone. Bring to boil, then reduce heat and simmer, covered, for 2 to 3 hours, or until beans begin to fall apart. Add remaining ingredients except for salt and pepper and simmer for 1 hour longer. Remove bone, cut meat off, and return meat to soup. Simmer for 3 more hours, stirring occasionally. Season to taste before serving.

Makes 4½ quarts.

Douglas Huntley
Cranston, Rhode Island

SPUR-OF-THE-MOMENT
SOUTH-OF-THE-BORDER SOUP

1 can (10½ ounces) bean
   with bacon soup
1 can (10½ ounces) tomato
   soup
1 can (10½ ounces) chili,
   with or without beans

1 soup can water
⅛ to ¼ teaspoon garlic
   powder
Corn chips or tortilla chips

☐ Stir soups, water, and garlic powder in a large saucepan. Heat
to boiling. Ladle soup into bowls and top with chips.
Makes 4 servings.

Dave's

Dave's Note: Could anything be easier?

GERMAN BEAN SOUP

My grandmother died in 1928 at the age of ninety-two, my
mother and father died in 1934 and 1935, and I am eighty-five
years of age. We have all been eating our bean soup made this
way and think there is nothing better. My parents were in their
seventies when they died. So you see, we have been using this
recipe for a good many years.

1 slice bread, preferably
   whole-wheat
1 cup cooked navy beans

2 cups whole milk
1 tablespoon butter
Salt and pepper to taste

☐ Cut bread into ½-inch squares. Place with all the other ingredients in a saucepan. Cook over medium heat and bring to a boil.
Remove from heat and serve. (Ingredients should be stirred frequently to keep from burning while cooking.)
Makes 2 servings.

Albert Helmuth
Gas City, Indiana

CAULIFLOWER AND BEAN SOUP

This soup was served in our home every Friday night along with a fillet of fried haddock (40 cents a pound). As children, we considered this a Depression meal. Forty years later we are still serving this combination, but now it's regarded as a nutritious alternative to meat and potatoes.

**1 package (10 ounces)
   frozen cauliflower
1 can (19 ounces) white
   cannellini beans,
   undrained**

**¼ cup olive oil
2 tablespoons chopped
   fresh parsley
Garlic flakes to taste
Salt and pepper to taste**

☐ Cook cauliflower as directed on package; do not drain. Add beans and season with olive oil, parsley, garlic, salt, and pepper. Simmer, covered, for 20 minutes.
   Makes 4 to 6 servings.

Ellie Knisley
Foxboro, Massachusetts

Dave's Note: I added a little more garlic the second time around.

LENTIL/SPINACH/NOODLE SOUP

**2 cups lentils
6 cups water
2 cloves minced garlic
3 tablespoons vegetable oil
2 cups wide noodles,
   broken**

**1 package (8 ounces)
   spinach, thoroughly
   cleaned
Salt and pepper to taste**

☐ Rinse and pick over lentils; cover with 6 cups water. Bring to a boil, then lower heat and simmer, covered, until lentils are soft, about 30 minutes. Sauté garlic in hot oil and add garlic and oil to lentils. Add noodles and spinach to mixture. Simmer until noodles are soft. Season to taste. Serve with garlic toast. Makes 4 to 6 servings.

Louise Dikmak
Allston, Massachusetts

VEGETARIAN SPLIT-PEA SOUP

1 cup green or yellow split
  peas
3 quarts water
2 carrots, pared and
  chopped
1 medium onion, chopped
1 large potato, pared and
  chopped
1 cup chopped spinach or
  broccoli

1 stalk celery, chopped, or
  ¼ teaspoon celery
  flakes
1½ teaspoons salt
¼ teaspoon black pepper
½ teaspoon garlic
  powder
Pinch of dried marjoram
1 tablespoon butter or
  margarine

☐ Soak peas in water overnight. Drain. Add 3 quarts water, the vegetables, seasonings, and butter. Bring to boil, then reduce heat and simmer, covered, until tender, about 1 to 1½ hours. Pour into blender or food processor and purée for about 5 seconds. Return to cooking pot and keep over low heat until ready to serve. Serve with garlic-flavored croutons or oyster crackers. Makes 6 servings.

Eugene J. Murphy
Dearborn Heights, Michigan

WHAT? ANOTHER SPLIT-PEA SOUP?

3 tablespoons butter
3 large onions
¼ cup chopped fresh
  parsley

3 tablespoons finely diced
  celery root or celery
  with leaves
6 cups water

2 medium russet potatoes,
   pared and finely diced
2 cups quick-cooking split
   peas, rinsed and drained
2 bay leaves, bruised
½ teaspoon freshly
   ground pepper
Generous pinch of ground
   cloves

1½ cups finely diced
   smoked ham, preferably
   country ham
1 cup beer
4 to 5 strips bacon,
   coarsely diced
Chicken stock (optional)
⅓ cup sour cream
Salt

☐ Melt butter in stockpot or large Dutch oven over medium-high heat. Dice 2 of the onions and add, along with the parsley and celery root. Cook, stirring constantly, until limp. Stir in water, potatoes, peas, bay leaves, pepper, and cloves and bring to a boil. Reduce heat to low and simmer, covered, stirring occasionally, for about 1 hour. Add ham and beer. Cover and cook, stirring occasionally, until peas are tender, adding more water if necessary to prevent sticking, about 1 hour.

Meanwhile, cook bacon in heavy medium skillet over high heat until almost crisp. Remove with slotted spoon and drain on paper towels. Discard all but 2 tablespoons of fat. Slice remaining onion into ⅛-inch rings. Add to fat in skillet and cook, stirring frequently, over medium heat until golden. Drain on paper towels.

Stir chicken stock into split-pea mixture if thinner consistency is desired and cook until heated through. Stir in sour cream. Remove from heat. Discard bay leaves and season with salt. Divide among heated individual soup plates or bowls. Top each with bacon and onion rings and serve.

Makes 4 to 5 servings.

Dave's

POTAGE SAINT-GERMAIN
(Fresh Pea Soup)

I got this recipe from my mother, who passed away this past February at age eighty-eight. She emigrated to this country in 1914, and like so many other girls went straight into household service (at $0.00 per week). She knew absolutely nothing about cooking or housekeeping and was taught everything from the ground up by her employer. Unfortunately, many of her "recipes" died with her, because there *were* no recipes. I was able to figure this one out and put it on paper. We used to call this her "show-off" soup because it seemed that she always made it when we had company she was trying to impress.

1 package (10 ounces) frozen peas
10 spinach leaves, thoroughly cleaned
10 lettuce leaves
1 can (10½ ounces) chicken broth
⅛ teaspoon pepper
½ cup chopped leek or scallion
½ teaspoon chopped fresh parsley
¾ cup light cream
2 tablespoons butter
Croutons

☐Put all the ingredients, except the cream, butter, and croutons, in a saucepan. Cover and simmer for 20 minutes. Pour into a blender or food processor; process until smooth. Sieve soup back into pan. Add cream and butter, then heat thoroughly but do not boil. Pour into bowls; sprinkle each serving with croutons.
    Makes 4 servings.

Katherine Laviolette
Cambridge, Massachusetts

CREAM OF FRESH PEA SOUP

3 pounds fresh peas, shelled (about 3 cups)
4 cups chicken stock
5 tablespoons unsalted butter
¼ cup all-purpose flour
4 cups milk, hot
1 teaspoon salt
¼ teaspoon freshly ground white pepper
Sugar (if necessary)

☐Place peas in freezer until hard, about 1 hour. Put frozen peas in a food processor fitted with metal blade or in blender; purée, using on/off motion and working in batches if necessary, until mixture resembles moist coarse meal. Set aside.

Make a roux by heating 3 tablespoons of the butter in a medium saucepan over medium heat; stir in flour until mixture is smooth. Cook for 3 minutes, stirring constantly. Gradually add milk in slow, steady stream, whisking constantly and scraping corners of pan to blend flour mixture thoroughly with the milk. Lower heat to simmer. Add salt and pepper. Simmer, uncovered, for 10 minutes, stirring occasionally.

Meanwhile, bring stock to a boil in a large saucepan and stir in pea puree. Reduce heat and simmer until peas are softened, about 4 minutes. Slowly whisk pea mixture into roux. Simmer, stirring occasionally, for 10 minutes. Taste and adjust seasonings, adding a little sugar if necessary. Strain soup through a sieve into large, warmed serving tureen. Swirl remaining 2 tablespoons butter into soup. Serve immediately.

Makes 8 servings.

Dave's

OLD-FASHIONED GERMAN SNIPPLED BEAN SOUP

Just a few lines about "snippled" bean soup. It is always made with fresh pork. Years ago this region of Ohio was known for the processing of pork, which was put on canal boats to be shipped to Cincinnati, an early, predominately German city. Germans were known for their sauerkraut, and I presume they tried souring green beans to have something different to cook with the pork. I remember my grandmother "snippling" the beans as a child and was fascinated how quickly she could do it. The name "snippled" comes from the diagonal cutting of the beans.

Green beans   Potatoes
Salt   Pepper
Fresh pork or ham

☐Measurements are up to you.

To make snippled beans, cut fresh green beans in ⅛-inch diagonal pieces. Put in a gallon crock in layers sprinkled with salt. Press tightly to form juice as with sauerkraut. Weight down and keep in a warm place until fermented, about 10 days to 2 weeks.

To prepare soup, take out enough beans for a meal and cook with any fresh pork (shoulder or ham is good). Add enough water to cover and enough potatoes, pared and cut in small cubes, to equal the beans. Season with salt and pepper. Simmer for several hours (add more water if necessary).

Ivolyn Bergman
Houston, Ohio

LENNIE'S FRENCH ONION SOUP

This is a recipe that was given to me by a gourmet friend who has done all the cooking on our strictly men's fishing weekends starting fifteen years ago. I have been making this soup at home also, which family and friends have enjoyed.

3 tablespoons butter
1 tablespoon peanut oil
1½ pounds thinly sliced
    Spanish onions
1 tablespoon salt
¼ teaspoon sugar
3 tablespoons all-purpose
    flour
2 quarts brown stock or 3
    cans (10½ ounces each)
    diluted beef bouillon

½ cup dry white wine
    (dry vermouth is good)
2 tablespoons Cognac
    (optional)
Slices of French bread
Thin slices of Gruyère
    cheese

☐Heat butter and oil in a large frying pan. Add onions and sauté over medium heat until soft and golden, approximately 15 minutes (do not burn onions). Raise heat slightly and add salt and sugar (sugar helps the onions brown); cook, stirring frequently, until onions are golden brown (again, don't let the onions burn), approximately 10 minutes. Add flour and cook for 3 minutes, stirring constantly.

In a separate pan bring stock or bouillon to a boil and add onions. Season to taste with wine and Cognac and simmer, partially covered, for 1 hour.

To serve, reheat, in individual bowls, in hot oven until bubbly, each serving topped with a slice of buttered French bread and a slice of gruyère cheese.

Makes 8 servings.

Robert W. Peterson
Wakefield, Massachusetts

Dave's Note: Onions need to be cooked slowly in butter and oil and then simmered in stock.

ONION SOUP

8 onions, sliced
6 tablespoons butter
2 tablespoons all-purpose flour
1½ quarts strong beef stock
1 cup Trebbiano white wine

1 bay leaf
Salt and pepper to taste
6 slices French bread, toasted
Slices of Swiss or Gruyère cheese
Grated Parmesan cheese

☐Sauté onions in butter until lightly browned, stirring frequently. Add flour and mix thoroughly. Add stock, wine, bay leaf, salt and pepper and simmer for another 10 minutes; remove bay leaf.

Preheat oven to 400°F.

Put soup into an earthenware casserole and top with toast and slices of Swiss or Gruyère cheese, then with Parmesan cheese. Bake for 20 minutes and serve.

Makes 8 servings.

Mrs. M. Damato
Framingham, Massachusetts

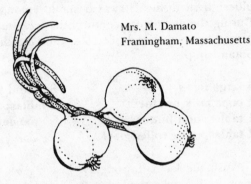

"LINNEA'S" ONION SOUP

I have served this delicious (and different) onion soup for many years, and everyone, including my eight grandchildren, have enjoyed each mouthful.

4 cups finely chopped onion
½ cup butter, plus additional for toast
5 chicken bouillon cubes
5 cups hot water

1 can (10½ ounces) chicken broth
1 cup heavy cream
Toast
Sharp cheese

☐Sauté onion in ½ cup butter until tender in a large saucepan. Dissolve bouillon cubes in hot water and add it and the broth to the onions. Cook for 20 minutes. Before serving, add cream and place a slice of buttered toast spread with sharp cheese on each soup bowl.

Makes 8 servings.

Muriel Minchin
Malden, Massachusetts

Dave's Note: I ate every bit. What a flavor!

BROTCHAN FOLTCHEP
(*Traditional Leek and Oatmeal Soup*)

Brotchan foltchep (pronounced Bro-hawn Fall-hep) is one of the oldest Irish dishes. It was a staple among the Celtic people. During the eighteenth century, the leeks and oatmeal were replaced by onions and potatoes, thus creating the famous Irish potato soup.

6 large leeks
4 cups milk or stock
1 tablespoon butter
2 tablespoons rolled oats

Salt and pepper
1 tablespoon chopped
   parsley

☐Wash the leeks thoroughly. Leaving on the green part, cut them into chunks about 1 inch long. Heat up the milk or stock with the butter, and when boiling add the oatmeal. Let it boil, then add the chopped leeks and season to taste. Cover, reduce heat, and simmer gently for 45 minutes. Add the parsley and bring to a boil again for a few minutes.
   Makes 4 servings.

James Garrett
Philadelphia, Pennsylvania

SCOTCH LEEK SOUP

I am a collector of cookbooks and recipes and have many unusual ones in my collection. I have been cooking since I was eight years old because I have always loved it. I never pursued it as a career, though I should have. My father died when I was six, leaving five children, the oldest was seven, so we were poor but didn't know it, since my mother took in laundry daily to feed us and we were never hungry. Anyway, the recipe that follows was a special Sunday dinner.
   Did you know that the leek is the flower of Scotland? On St.

David's day, a true Scot was seen wearing a leek in the brim of his hat as an ornament. Anyway, I'm sending you a true recipe for Scotch leek soup.

1 bunch leeks, thoroughly
   cleaned, trimmed, and
   cut in thin slices
1 cup thinly sliced celery
5 tablespoons butter

4 cups milk
2 cups pared cubed (1 inch)
   potatoes
Salt and pepper to taste
Cayenne pepper to taste

☐Cook leeks and celery in butter in top of double boiler until soft. Add milk and cook for 40 minutes over simmering water. Boil potatoes in another pan in salted water for 10 minutes. Add to the leek mixture and continue cooking until potatoes are soft. Season with salt, pepper, and cayenne pepper to taste.
   Makes 4 servings.

Mrs. Omar Van Gorp
Livonia, Michigan

Dave's Note: Mrs. V.G. serves this with chopped parsley and buttered croutons.

HOT TOMATO BISQUE

5 tablespoons butter
6 cups cut-up fresh, ripe
   tomatoes
4 slices dry bread, cubed
1½ teaspoons salt
¼ teaspoon freshly
   ground pepper

3 cloves garlic
6 cups water
1½ cups heavy cream
Very small pinch of dried
   basil
2 egg yolks
Buttered croutons

☐Heat butter in soup pot. Add tomatoes and cover. Simmer for 5 minutes, then add dry bread cubes, salt, and pepper. Mash garlic with side of knife, peel, and add to tomatoes along with the water. Bring to a boil. Cover and simmer for 1 hour. Process through a food mill to strain and return to soup pot; add basil and simmer for another hour.

Gradually beat cream into egg yolks and add mixture to tomato stock, beating constantly. Heat thoroughly, but don't let it boil. Serve with croutons.

Makes 10 to 12 servings.

Note: If tomatoes tend to be acidy, add a small amount of sugar to taste. Although not nearly as good, if fresh garden tomatoes are not available add 1 small can of tomato paste to improve flavor.

Eileen A. Harrington
Cortland, New York

Dave's Note: Good!

SWEET/SOUR TOMATO SOUP

1 can (16 ounces) tomato purée
1 can (10½ ounces) beef consommé
½ cup sugar
2 tablespoons vinegar
2 teaspoons salt

1 teaspoon Worcestershire sauce
Few grains of paprika
Few grains of celery salt
Onion juice to taste
Sour cream

☐ Mix all of the ingredients except the sour cream in a large saucepan and heat to the boiling point. Garnish with dollops of sour cream.

Makes 4 servings.

Dave's

FREEZER TOMATO SOUP

7 to 8 pounds (about 16 to 18 large) fresh, fully ripe tomatoes, chopped (about 12 cups)
3 large (about 2 pounds) onions, finely chopped
¼ cup sugar
¼ cup chopped parsley

6 tablespoons cornstarch dissolved in 6 tablespoons water
Salt and pepper to taste
Pinch of ground cloves (optional)
Butter (or margarine) or sour cream

☐In a 6- to 8-quart kettle, combine tomatoes, onions, sugar, and parsley. Cook over medium heat, stirring often, until tomatoes make enough juice and come to a boil. Reduce heat to medium-low and cover the kettle. Continue cooking for 45 minutes, stirring occasionally. Stir cornstarch mixture into tomato mixture. Cook, stirring, until mixture boils and thickens. Remove from heat and press part of the mixture at a time through a food mill or wire strainer. Discard seeds and pulp. Cool, then pack purée in pint-size freezer containers, allowing about 1 inch head space. Freeze.

To serve, thaw soup, pour into a pan, and stir over medium heat until hot. Add salt, pepper, and cloves to taste. Top each serving of soup with a small pat of butter or a spoonful of sour cream.

Makes about 12 cups (enough for 12 servings).

To make cream of tomato soup, add 1 cup milk or half-and-half and ½ teaspoon dried basil to each pint of thawed freezer tomato soup. Heat and serve.

To make tomato and broth soup, add 1 cup chicken broth and ¼ teaspoon dried thyme leaves to each pint of thawed freezer tomato soup. Heat and serve.

Dave's

SUPER TOMATO SOUP

You can make large quantities when tomatoes are plentiful and freeze—enjoy all winter.

12 cups chopped fresh,
   ripe tomatoes
6 onions, thinly sliced
8 cups water
½ cup sugar
4 teaspoons salt
½ teaspoon pepper

40 whole cloves
Chopped fresh parsley to
   taste
6 tablespoons butter
6 tablespoons cornstarch
Salted whipped cream

☐Combine tomatoes, onions, the water, sugar, salt, pepper, cloves, and parsley in soup pot. Heat to boiling, then reduce heat and simmer, covered, until onions and tomatoes are thoroughly cooked. Put through a sieve. Add butter. Dissolve cornstarch in a little water and add to soup pot. Boil, stirring, until slightly thickened. Serve hot. Garnish each serving with a tablespoon of salted whipped cream.

Makes about 4 quarts.

Alice McNutt
Boylston, Massachusetts

OLD-FASHIONED TOMATO SOUP

4 tablespoons vegetable oil
2 pearl onions, finely
   chopped, or 1 medium
   yellow onion, finely
   chopped
2 pounds fresh, ripe
   tomatoes, unpeeled,
   sliced
1 tablespoon tomato paste

1 bay leaf
½ teaspoon finely
   chopped garlic
2 teaspoons cornstarch or
   potato flour
3 cups chicken stock or
   vegetable stock
Freshly ground pepper to
   taste

Herb or vegetable salt to
taste
1 medium fresh, ripe
tomato, peeled, seeded
and cut in julienne

1 tablespoon finely
chopped fresh parsley
1 tablespoon finely
chopped chives
1 teaspoon light honey

☐Heat 3 tablespoons of the oil in a heavy 4-quart saucepan over
medium heat. Add onions and cook until translucent, about 5
minutes. Add sliced tomatoes and continue cooking for 3 minutes. Stir in tomato paste, bay leaf, and garlic. Cover and cook for
10 minutes, stirring often. Transfer mixture to a processor or
blender (in batches) and purée. (Or push through a fine strainer.)
Return purée to saucepan. Combine cornstarch and remaining
1 tablespoon oil in small bowl. Stir into purée. Add stock and
bring to a boil over medium heat, stirring constantly. Reduce
heat to low and simmer, uncovered, for 10 minutes. Season with
pepper and herb salt to taste. Stir in tomato julienne, parsley,
chives, and honey. Serve immediately or let cool, cover, and
refrigerate.
Makes 4 to 6 servings.

Dave's

*Dave's Note: If any is left over, add a little red wine vinegar, some chopped
green pepper and Bermuda onion, and croutons. Presto, gaspacho.*

CREAM OF FRESH TOMATO SOUP

4 tablespoons vegetable oil
1 medium yellow onion,
finely chopped
½ teaspoon finely
chopped garlic
6 medium fresh, ripe
tomatoes, unpeeled
2 tablespoons tomato paste
2 tablespoons whole-wheat
pastry flour

2 cups (or more) chicken
stock or vegetable stock
¾ cup half-and-half or
double-strength,
reconstituted nonfat dry
milk
Herb or vegetable salt to
taste
2 tablespoons finely
chopped chives

☐Heat 2 tablespoons of the oil in a heavy 4-quart saucepan over low heat. Add onion and garlic and sauté for 1 minute. Slice 5 of the tomatoes and add to the skillet; sauté, stirring constantly, for 5 minutes. Remove from heat.

Combine tomato paste, flour, and remaining 2 tablespoons oil in small bowl and mix well. Stir into tomato mixture. Add 2 cups stock and bring to a boil over medium heat, stirring constantly. Remove from heat. Transfer mixture to processor or blender (in batches) and purée (or press through fine strainer).

Return purée to saucepan. Place over low heat and cook, uncovered, for 15 minutes. Add half-and-half. Stir in more stock if thinner consistency is desired. Season with herb salt to taste. Peel and seed remaining tomato; cut flesh into julienne. Stir into soup along with chives and warm through. Serve right away.

Makes 3 to 4 servings.

Dave's

CREAM OF TOMATO AND POTATO SOUP

6 tablespoons vegetable oil
4 large potatoes, pared and sliced
2 medium yellow onions, sliced
1 cup water
1 cup milk or double-strength, reconstituted nonfat dry milk
2 teaspoons finely chopped garlic

1 pound ripe tomatoes, unpeeled, sliced
3 tablespoons tomato paste
¼ teaspoon ground sage
¼ cup (or more) half-and-half or double-strength, reconstituted nonfat dry milk
Herb or vegetable salt
2 tablespoons finely chopped fresh parsley

☐Heat 2 tablespoons of the oil in a heavy 4-quart saucepan over low heat. Add potatoes, half of sliced onion, the water, milk, and garlic. Cover and cook until potatoes are soft. Set aside.

Heat remaining oil in large skillet. Add sliced tomatoes, tomato paste, remaining onion, and sage. Cover and cook until tomatoes are soft, about 10 to 12 minutes. Add to potato mixture, blending well. Transfer mixture to a processor or blender (in batches) and purée (or press through fine strainer). Return puree to saucepan and stir in ¼ cup half-and-half, adding more if soup seems too thick. Season with herb salt to taste. Place over low heat and heat through, or let cool, cover and refrigerate. Garnish each serving with chopped parsley.

Makes 4 to 6 servings, hot or cold.

Dave's

DELICIOUS POTATO SOUP

8 slices bacon, diced
⅓ cup green onion, white part only
1 cup chopped celery or ½ cup cream of celery soup
1 package (10 ounces) frozen hash brown potatoes

1 can (10½ ounces) condensed cream of chicken soup or cream of celery soup
5 cups milk
1½ teaspoons salt
⅛ teaspoon white pepper

☐Fry bacon until crisp in a large saucepan. Remove from pan to drain. Add green onion and sauté until transparent. Remove onion from pan and drain off all but 1 tablespoon of bacon fat. Add celery and cook until crisp yet tender. Add potatoes, soup, milk, salt, and pepper. Add reserved bacon and onion and simmer slowly, uncovered; for 10 minutes. Stir occasionally until thickened.

Makes 8 servings.

Mrs. Edna Macartney
Lorain, Ohio

Dave's Note: Really good. I preferred cream of chicken soup.

POTATO SOUP

This is written as it appears in my mother's 1906 *Ladies of the Universalist Society Cook Book*. So easy and so good.

3 large potatoes
1 pint milk
1 teaspoon chopped onion
1 stalk celery
1 teaspoon salt
½ teaspoon celery salt

½ teaspoon white pepper
¼ teaspoon cayenne
   pepper
½ teaspoon flour
1 tablespoon butter

☐Wash and pare potatoes and let them soak in cold water for half an hour. Put them in boiling water and cook until they are soft. Cook the onion and celery with the milk in a double boiler. When the potatoes are soft, drain off the water and wash them. Add the boiling milk and season. Rub through a strainer and put it on to boil again. Put the butter in a small saucepan and when melted and bubbling add the flour and when well mixed, stir into boiling soup. Boil 5 minutes and serve very hot. Season to taste.
   Makes 4 servings.

Mrs. Aimo J. Sulin
Rockland, Maine

POTATO AND MUSHROOM SOUP

This potato and mushroom soup comes from Poland. My mother used to make it for us. It's more than eighty years old. In Poland they call this soup *zmiocanka*. The soup was usually prepared on Fridays when consumption of meat was forbidden.

2 carrots, pared and cut up
1 stalk of celery, cut up
1 onion, chopped

1 clove garlic, chopped
1 teaspoon chopped fresh
   parsley

4 to 5 quarts water
2 beef bouillon cubes
4 to 5 potatoes, pared and
   cut up
½ teaspoon margarine or
   butter
½ teaspoon melted salt
   pork

Salt and pepper to taste
1 teaspoon soy sauce
5 or more fresh
   mushrooms, sliced
Few dashes of vegetable oil
2 to 3 tablespoons
   all-purpose flour

☐Put the carrots, celery, onion, garlic, and parsley in a large pot
containing 4 to 5 quarts water; add bouillon cubes. Cook the
vegetables until they are tender. Add potatoes, margarine, salt
pork, salt and pepper to taste, and soy sauce. Cook for 5 to 10
minutes more until potatoes are done.

In a small saucepan, sauté mushrooms in oil until done; add to
soup. In another saucepan, add flour and let it get brown, stirring
it, and add approximately 1 cup of water or more to make a
gravy-like sauce. Add this to soup. Stir and let simmer for about
5 minutes or more.

Makes about 16 servings.

Mrs. Edward Kivior
Ludlow, Massachusetts

SOPA DE CALABACITAS
(Zucchini Soup)

As the old-timers of New England used to say of their clam
chowder, "It's even tastier if allowed to 'ripen' overnight in the
refrigerator!" I make large batches of this soup, eat some, and
freeze servings in Seal-A-Meal bags. Serve it with garlic-buttered
Italian bread and grated Parmesan cheese.

8 to 10 Italian sweet
   sausages
2 cups sliced celery, cut on
   an angle in ½-inch
   pieces

2 pounds zucchini, sliced in
   ½-inch pieces
1 cup chopped onion
2 cans (28 ounces each)
   tomatoes, with liquid

2 teaspoons salt
1 teaspoon Italian
   seasoning
1 teaspoon dried oregano
1 teaspoon sugar
½ teaspoon dried basil

¼ teaspoon garlic
   powder
2 large green peppers,
   seeded and cut into
   ½-inch pieces

☐Remove skin from sausages; cut each one into 4 sections and shape into balls. Brown sausage balls in a large Dutch oven, heavy skillet, or 6-quart pressure cooker. Drain off excess fat and set sausage aside. Simmer celery, zucchini and onion in fat remaining in Dutch oven for 10 minutes, stirring occasionally. Add all the remaining ingredients, except green peppers. Simmer, covered, for about 20 to 30 minutes. Add green peppers and cook, covered, for 10 minutes, or until squash and peppers are tender. Makes 3½ quarts.

Mrs. R.W. Howe
Stoneham, Massachusetts

Dave's Note: Mr. Howe writes: "My wife, Phyllis, who apparently submitted the recipe, is no longer with us, having died in January of this year. I am sure she would give her permission to use the recipe as you see fit, so I have signed for her. To the best of my knowledge, this recipe was obtained in Spain by my daughter when she spent a college semester there in 1972."

SUNSHINE SOUP

This recipe was invented during the war when meat was not available. When my children were small, and it rained, they weren't allowed to go out. So they sulked a bit. One day I started an omelet, and when the zucchini and onion were sautéed, I added a little water, then beat in the eggs, cheese and parsley. It was like a broth when I served it, and I said we were having sunshine in our house in our soup. They loved it. It was passed onto the grandchildren and now the great-grandchildren.

2 medium zucchini
1 medium onion, chopped
Vegetable oil
Salt and pepper to taste
2 eggs

½ teaspoon finely
   chopped fresh parsley
2 tablespoons grated
   Parmesan cheese
Garlic powder to taste

☐Wash and dry zucchini. Cut off ends. Cut in 2-inch-long, ½-inch-wide strips. Sauté the chopped onion in a little vegetable oil. When onions are soft but not brown, add the zucchini and salt and pepper. Cover with water and cook, uncovered, on medium heat until tender (do not overcook).

While this is cooking, beat eggs with parsley, grated parmesan cheese and a little garlic powder. Mix this into the zucchini mixture with a fork. Add a little more water, just enough to make a broth. Serve hot, with French bread and butter.

Makes 4 servings.

Mary LaFozia
Bristol, Rhode Island

SUMMER SQUASH SOUP

2 pounds yellow summer
   squash, cut in ½-inch
   slices
1 large onion, diced
6 cups chicken broth
Dash of salt and pepper

2 tablespoons all-purpose
   flour
½ cup cream or milk
Dash of nutmeg
1 slice bread, toasted and
   cubed

☐Cook squash and onions in chicken broth (set aside approximately 2 tablespoons broth), simmering slowly until soft, about 10 minutes. Put mixture in blender and purée until smooth and seeds are all chopped. Mix salt, pepper and flour in the reserved broth and add to purée. Return mixture to heat and simmer until it thickens slightly. Add cream and heat just to boiling, do not boil. Add a dash of nutmeg and serve garnished with toast cubes.

This also may be served cold.

Makes 6 servings.

Carlee L. Howe
Burlington, Massachusetts

Dave's Note: Mild-mannered but nice. Be sure to add liberal amounts of salt and pepper.

PUMPKIN SOUP

It is quite an experience if you are eating this soup for the first time. It does not taste like pumpkin. Delicious.

9 tablespoons butter
2 pounds onion, thinly
  sliced
4 cloves garlic, peeled and
  chopped
2½ pounds diced pared
  fresh pumpkin

6 cups chicken stock
Salt to taste
1 large stalk celery,
  chopped
3 tablespoons all-purpose
  flour

☐Melt 7 tablespoons of butter in a large saucepan and sauté onion and garlic until golden. Add pumpkin, chicken stock, salt, and celery. Bring to a boil and then simmer until pumpkin is soft and well cooked, about 30 minutes. Blend soup in a blender or with a hand mixer until the pumpkin is completely dissolved. Return to pan. Knead flour with remaining 2 tablespoons butter, softened, and gradually add it to the soup, beating with a whisk. Bring soup to a boil, whisking until it thickens. Correct seasonings and serve.

Makes 8 servings.

Veronica McKinnon
Kirkland Lake, Ontario, Canada

Dave's Note: You can use canned pumpkin, but the soup is best made with fresh.

CURRIED PUMPKIN SOUP

2 tablespoons butter
¼ cup finely chopped
  onion
1 tablespoon all-purpose
  flour
1½ teaspoons curry
  powder
2 cans (10¾ ounces)
  chicken broth
1 can (16 ounces) pumpkin

1 teaspoon brown sugar
¼ teaspoon salt
Freshly ground pepper to
  taste
Freshly grated nutmeg to
  taste
1 cup milk
Minced fresh chives or
  parsley
Low-fat plain yogurt

☐Melt butter in a heavy 3-quart saucepan over medium-high heat. Add onion and sauté until translucent, about 5 minutes. Mix in flour and curry powder and cook until bubbly, about 2 minutes. Remove from heat and gradually stir in broth. Add pumpkin, brown sugar, salt, pepper, and nutmeg. Cook over medium heat, stirring constantly, until thickened. Blend in milk and continue cooking until warmed through; do not boil. Ladle into bowls. Sprinkle with chives or parsley and garnish with yogurt. Serve immediately.
  Makes 6 to 8 servings.

Dave's

VELVETY PUMPKIN BISQUE

1 tablespoon minced green
  onion
2 tablespoons butter
1 can (16 ounces) pumpkin
1 cup water
2 teaspoons brown sugar
½ teaspoon salt
⅛ teaspoon white pepper

⅛ teaspoon ground
  cinnamon
2 chicken bouillon cubes or
  envelopes
2 cups half-and-half
1 lemon, thinly sliced, or
  minced fresh parsley

☐Prepare 30 minutes before serving. In a 2-quart saucepan over medium heat, sauté green onion in butter until tender. Stir in remaining ingredients, except for half-and-half and lemon or parsley, until blended and mixture begins to boil. Cook for 5 minutes to blend flavors. Stir in half-and-half and heat through. Garnish with lemon slice or parsley.

Makes about 5 cups, or 10 first-course servings.

Dave's

Dave's Note: I'm not too crazy about pumpkin anything (well, chiffon pie maybe) but this is very pleasant.

ALL-WEATHER BROCCOLI SOUP

4 cups chopped fresh broccoli
2 cups chicken broth
1 small onion, quartered
1 clove garlic, halved

1 teaspoon fresh lemon juice
Salt and freshly ground pepper to taste
Lemon slices

☐Combine broccoli, broth, onion, and garlic in a large saucepan over medium-high heat and cook, uncovered, until broccoli is tender, about 10 to 15 minutes. Transfer to a blender in batches and purée until smooth. Return to saucepan. Add lemon juice and season with salt and pepper. Cook until heated through. Ladle soup into bowls and garnish with lemon slices.

Makes 4 servings.

Dave's

Dave's Note: Soup can also be served cold with a dollop of plain yogurt.

CREAM OF BROCCOLI AND
MUSHROOM SOUP

3 stalks broccoli (or 4 cups
    of tops)
1 cup sliced fresh
    mushrooms
3 tablespoons butter
2 cups chicken stock or 1
    can (10¾ ounces)
    chicken broth
1 tablespoon chopped fresh
    parsley

¼ teaspoon dried
    tarragon
⅛ teaspoon ground
    coriander
Salt and pepper to taste
1 tablespoon all-purpose
    flour
1 cup heavy cream
Nutmeg

☐Cut up stems and tops of broccoli. Bring 4 quarts of water to a boil and dump in all of the broccoli. Cook, uncovered, until soft, then drain and let cool slightly. Slice mushrooms and sauté in 1 tablespoon of the butter until golden in color. Set aside.

Heat broth and add parsley, tarragon, coriander, salt and pepper. Separate out 1½ cups of broccoli tops and set aside. Purée rest of broccoli with mushrooms and enough broth to make it smooth. Pour mixture into remaining broth and simmer for 20 minutes.

In a separate saucepan, melt remaining 2 tablespoons butter and add flour, stirring constantly; add to soup. Break apart reserved broccoli tops and add to soup. Add the cream and heat through. Before serving, garnish with nutmeg.

Makes 4 servings.

Note: If you use canned broth, use the water you cooked broccoli in to dilute the concentrate.

Beatrice Susser
Little Silver, New Jersey

MUSHROOM SOUP

1 pound mushrooms, sliced
3 tablespoons butter
Dash of nutmeg
1 small onion, finely
  chopped
3 tablespoons all-purpose
  flour
½ teaspoon salt
¼ teaspoon black pepper

⅛ teaspoon dried
  oregano
⅛ teaspoon cayenne
  pepper
2 chicken bouillon cubes
2 beef bouillon cubes
3¾ cups water
1 bay leaf
1 cup heavy cream

☐Sauté mushrooms in 2 tablespoons of the butter with a dash of nutmeg and set aside. Melt remaining 1 tablespoon butter in pot. After foam subsides, add onion and sauté, stirring occasionally, for 5 to 7 minutes, until soft and translucent but not brown. Remove pot from heat. With wooden spoon, stir in flour, salt, pepper, oregano, and cayenne to make a smooth paste. Gradually stir in stock made of bouillon cubes dissolved in the water, being careful to avoid lumps. Stir in mushrooms and add bay leaf. Return pot to heat and bring to a boil, stirring constantly. Reduce heat, cover, and simmer for 30 minutes. Uncover pan and stir in cream. Reheat soup, stirring constantly, for 2 to 3 minutes or until hot. Do not boil. Remove from heat, remove bay leaf, and serve.
  Makes 4 servings.

Eileen A. Harrington
Cortland, New York

MAINE EGGPLANT SUPPER SOUP

Too lazy to cook eggplant Parmesan one afternoon, I fooled around with a few recipes and arrived at one that was easy and delicious. I serve it with garlic bread and tossed salad and dessert. Super supper.

1 **pound ground beef**	1 **can (28 ounces) tomatoes**
1 **medium onion, chopped**	1½ **teaspoons salt**
1 **stalk celery, chopped**	½ **teaspoon pepper**
1 **large carrot, pared and**	¼ **teaspoon nutmeg**
sliced	¼ **teaspoon garlic powder**
1 **large eggplant, pared and**	2 **teaspoons sugar**
diced	1 **cup water**
3 **beef bouillon cubes**	½ **cup macaroni**
dissolved in 3 cups	2 **tablespoons chopped**
water	**fresh parsley**
1 **bay leaf**	

☐Brown beef and onion in a large saucepan. Add remaining ingredients, except macaroni and parsley, and simmer, covered, for 30 minutes. Skim off any excess fat. Add macaroni and parsley. Cook for 10 minutes longer, or until macaroni is done. Makes 6 servings.

Ellie Lashua
Kennebunk, Maine

Dave's Note: Very hearty, thick, and satisfying.

CORN-TOMATO CHOWDER

This recipe was a favorite of my mother's and dates back, at least, to 1926 when, as a bride, I wrote it in my first cookbook. This recipe can be made with fresh corn and tomatoes, but I prefer to make it with canned cream-style corn and tomatoes as suggested in my recipe. The cream-style corn and evaporated milk gives it a creamier appearance and flavor. It is different from the usual run-of-the-mill chowders.

2 **medium onions, chopped**	2½ **cups cubed potatoes**
1 **large green pepper,**	4 **cups water**
seeded and chopped	1 **teaspoon salt**

Pepper to taste	**⅛ teaspoon baking soda**
1 can (16 ounces)	**1 can (13 ounces)**
cream-style corn	**evaporated milk**
2 cups chopped stewed	
tomatoes	

☐Combine first 6 ingredients. Boil gently in a covered 4-quart kettle for 20 to 25 minutes, until vegetables are tender. Add corn and tomatoes and heat thoroughly. Add baking soda (this is important to keep the milk and tomatoes from curdling). Scald milk and add to the kettle. Serve hot, with crisp crackers and a dollop of butter.

Makes 8 servings.

Marion Cassie
Dedham, Massachusetts

CORN CHOWDER MEDLEY

½ cup thinly sliced	**1 can (10½ ounces) cream**
onion	**of mushroom soup**
2 tablespoons margarine	**2½ cups milk**
1 cup diced cooked	**¾ teaspoon salt**
potatoes	**Dash of pepper**
1 cup diced cooked ham	**Chopped fresh parsley**
1 can (16 ounces)	**(optional)**
cream-style corn	

☐In a 4-quart saucepan, sauté onion in margarine until soft. Add all the remaining ingredients except parsley. Bring to a boil and serve. May be sprinkled with chopped parsley when served.

Makes 8 servings.

Mildred Bassett
Alexandria, Indiana

POLISH BORSCHT

Borscht is an Easter dish for the Polish people, but it is good anytime. This is a recipe I put together myself about twenty-five years ago, and I am still using it. Before that I tried all kinds of borscht recipes but was never satisfied, mostly because the original borscht is made by combining rye flour or oatmeal with water and fermenting it for several days to make the sour-tasting juice. I didn't want to wait that long, so I decided to experiment with vinegar until I came up with something I liked.

1 smoked sausage	3 cups milk
4 cloves garlic, chopped	8 hard-boiled eggs, sliced
5 teaspoons salt	2 bunches beets, cooked
8 tablespoons vinegar	⅔ cup all-purpose flour

☐Boil sausage in water. Remove sausage and cut in slices and return to kettle with liquid. If you don't have 2 quarts, add more water. Add remaining ingredients, except flour. Mix flour with enough water to make a paste and add to kettle. Bring to a boil and shut off heat.

Serve borscht in soup plates, accompanied by buttered mashed potatoes made with sautéed onion.

Note: You can use raw sausage. If you do, first fry it and then transfer with drippings to the kettle of water.

Makes about 12 servings.

Winifred Kiwak
Webster, Massachusetts

CREAM OF CARROT SOUP

4 tablespoons butter	2 cups evaporated milk
4 cups sliced pared carrots	1 cup whole milk
2 cups sliced onion	2 teaspoons salt
1 clove garlic, crushed	1 teaspoon white pepper

1 teaspoon sugar	Chopped fresh parsley
2 egg yolks	Croutons
Pinch of nutmeg	

☐Heat butter in saucepan and add carrots, onion, and garlic. Cover and cook over low heat for 15 minutes, stirring occasionally. Blend or put through food mill to purée. Bring to a simmer again and add milk, salt, pepper, and sugar. Beat egg yolks with a little of the purée, then gradually stir egg mixture into soup. Bring to a boil and remove from stove. Add nutmeg and garnish with parsley; serve with croutons.
Makes 6 to 8 servings.

Nancy Dunn
Pomfret Center, Connecticut

CREAM OF ASPARAGUS SOUP WITH GRUYÈRE

1 pound asparagus, trimmed and pared	Salt and freshly ground white pepper to taste
2 tablespoons unsalted butter	½ cup half-and-half
1¾ cups chicken stock or broth	1 egg yolk
	¼ cup grated Gruyère cheese

☐Blanch asparagus until crisp-tender, about 4 minutes. Rinse under cold running water and drain. Reserve 6 of the asparagus tips for garnish. Sauté remaining asparagus in butter in a large saucepan over medium heat until tender. Transfer to a food processor or blender and purée. Mix puree and stock in a saucepan. Heat over low heat to barely simmering. Season to taste with salt and pepper. Whisk together half-and-half, egg yolk, and cheese in a small bowl. Whisk into soup. Heat just until slightly thickened and soup is warm. Garnish with reserved asparagus tips. Season to taste.

Makes about 4 cups.

Dave's

Dave's Note: Smart idea to serve right away.

CREAM OF BELL PEPPER SOUP

4 green peppers, seeded and diced

8 ounces sorrel leaves, finely chopped, or 8 ounces spinach

Juice of ½ lemon (or 1 lemon if spinach is used)

4 cups or more chicken stock

3 shallots, finely chopped

1 teaspoon finely chopped fresh chives

1 teaspoon salt

¼ teaspoon white pepper

3 tablespoons butter

3 tablespoons all-purpose flour

½ to ⅔ cup half-and-half

☐Combine peppers, sorrel, and lemon juice in a bowl; set aside. In a medium saucepan, heat 4 cups stock until simmering. Add pepper-sorrel mixture, shallots, chives, salt, and pepper. Cover and simmer for 30 minutes. Transfer vegetables to a blender with enough of the cooking liquid to cover; reserve remaining liquid. Purée until completely smooth.

To make roux, melt butter in a medium saucepan. Stir in flour and cook until light golden. Add reserved liquid and puréed vegetables. Return to a boil, then reduce heat and simmer for 10 minutes, stirring constantly. Remove from heat and let cool slightly. Add half-and-half. Strain through a fine sieve; discard pulp. Thin with additional chicken stock if desired.

Makes 6 servings.

Dave's

CANADIAN CHEESE SOUP

The outstanding thought that comes to mind when I think of this and other dairy delicacies is that I could not make them when my husband was in town. "At no time in my home, in my presence will you serve cheese" (Real Roquefort excepted). That rule I accepted when I took the marital plunge with a stubborn (he was) New Englander who apparently had been served a sufficiency or so of C-rations during his infantry years and five invasions in W.W. II before I met him. However, he traveled a great deal, so the rest of us ate a great deal of cheese.

The recipe serves 6, but be prepared for extra servings—they'll come back for more. For the men's poker game party, serve with crusty chunks of bread, salad, and beer. For lunch or after theater, substitute white wine for the beer.

3 tablespoons grated pared
    carrot
3 tablespoons butter
3 tablespoons grated onion
4 cups chicken broth
½ teaspoon dry mustard
½ tablespoon paprika
2 tablespoons cornstarch

¼ cup milk
¼ pound (1 cup grated)
    cheddar cheese (you
    decide—mild, medium,
    or old)
1 cup beer
Chopped fresh parsley

☐Sauté carrot and onion in butter until soft. Add chicken broth, mustard, and paprika. Continue to cook over low heat for about 15 minutes. Mix cornstarch with milk and add to soup. Remove from heat and cool for about 5 minutes. Add cheese and beer and return to heat. Stir over low heat until cheese melts. Serve with a sprinkling of parsley.

Makes 6 servings.

Dorothea S. Mason
Chatham, Ontario, Canada

Dave's Note: I'll add here that the white wine as a substitute for the beer is not to be ignored.

CIDER SOUP

This is a Pennsylvania German dish, and I found it in a recipe book more than fifty years ago.

6 cups cider
½ cup plus 2 tablespoons
  sugar
2 cups cubed bread
Butter

2 eggs
2 tablespoons all-purpose
  flour
1½ cups milk
Whole allspice

☐ Boil cider; skim; stir in the ½ cup sugar. Brown cubed bread in a little butter. Beat eggs well in a small bowl and add the 2 tablespoons sugar, the flour, milk, and allspice. Add egg mixture to cider. Stir browned bread into mixture last.
Makes 6 servings.

Geraldine Fuhrman
Hanover, Pennsylvania

WINE SOUP

3½ cups sweet red wine
1½ cups water
3 tablespoons lemon
  juice

4 eggs
5 tablespoons sugar
1 teaspoon salt

☐ Combine wine, water, and lemon juice in a saucepan. Bring to a boil and cook, uncovered, over low heat for 10 minutes. Beat 2 of the eggs and 2 egg yolks (reserving the 2 egg whites). Add 3 tablespoons of the sugar and the salt. Gradually add the wine mixture, stirring constantly to prevent curdling. Chill.

Before serving, beat the egg whites until they begin to stiffen. Add the remaining 2 tablespoons sugar gradually, beating constantly until stiff. Serve the soup with a heaping tablespoon of the egg white meringue on top.

Makes 4 servings.

Dave's

Dave's Note: Tastes more like a dessert.

POPCORN SOUP
(Pretz Soup)

1 egg	2 hard-boiled egg yolks,
1 cup all-purpose flour	grated
5 cups milk	2½ cups popped popcorn
2 tablespoons butter	Dash of cayenne pepper
2 teaspoons chopped fresh	Salt (optional)
parsley	

☐Beat egg. Sift flour and blend into egg, chopping lightly with a spatula until mixture flakes into lumps. Bring milk to a boil and add butter; reduce heat and simmer. Drop lumps of flour and egg into the milk, a few at a time, stirring until the lumps are cooked, about 10 minutes. Add parsley and grated egg yolks.

Divide the popcorn among 4 large bowls. Pour soup on top and sprinkle with cayenne pepper (and salt if needed). Serve at once.

Makes 4 servings.

Robert Capobianco
Lawrence, Massachusetts

BUTTER BALL SOUP

8 slices day-old bread	3 cans (10½ ounces each)
3 tablespoons soft butter	chicken broth
1 egg	1 tablespoon chopped fresh
¼ teaspoon salt	parsley
⅛ teaspoon white pepper	

☐Remove crust from bread and crumble bread between hands to make fine crumbs. Add butter, egg, salt, and pepper. Mix well and knead until mixture can be formed into balls. Make about 30 ½-inch balls. Drop into boiling broth and simmer for 10 minutes. Sprinkle with parsley.

Makes 6 servings.

Mrs. Louise Cercone
Walpole, Massachusetts

PEANUT BUTTER SOUP

I made this soup up one day as I came out of the garden from weeding all day, rather tired, knowing that my mother, who was still alive then, liked all soups and stews, so this soup came to me on the spur of the moment. Since my mother had just taken some loaves of rye bread out of the oven, we had a super dinner before I went out to milk her cow.

1 cup water	¼ cup peanut butter
1 onion, chopped	1 tablespoon butter
3 cups milk	4 pieces crisp bacon

☐Boil onion in water until tender. Add milk and peanut butter. Cook slowly, stirring continually so that it won't boil over, for a few minutes. Add butter and serve with crisp bacon pieces crumbled on top.

Makes 4 servings.

Betty Underwood
Fitchburg, Massachusetts

DANDELION CREAM SOUP

¼ cup butter
3 tablespoons all-purpose
    flour
1 cup finely chopped
    dandelion greens
    (uncooked)

1 clove garlic, minced
3 shoots chives, minced
1 teaspoon salt
Pinch of pepper
1 cup milk

☐Melt butter in a saucepan over low heat. Add flour, stirring to a smooth paste. Add greens, garlic, chives, salt, and pepper and sauté for 3 to 4 minutes. Gradually add milk, stirring over low heat until smoothly blended and slightly thickened. Let simmer for 5 minutes longer and serve.

Makes 2 servings.

Mrs. Sylvia F. Coffin
Plymouth, Massachusetts

DANISH FRUIT SOUP

It is strange, but my mother, who was the product of Irish immigrants on both sides, turned out a better Danish cook than all of my grandmother's blood daughters. My grandmother loved to come to visit us because my mother was an extraordinary cook, and my grandmother, above all else, loved to eat! She was enormous and never would tell anyone her exact weight, but it evidently didn't do her any harm, because she lived until the ripe old age of ninety-six, eating heartily to the end.

4 cups water
1 stick cinnamon
2 cups mixed cut-up fruit
    of your choice
1 tablespoon cornstarch

¼ cup quick-cooking
    tapioca
½ cup sugar
1 tablespoon lemon juice

☐Combine water, cinnamon, and fruit in a saucepan and boil for 5 minutes. Add a small amount of cold water to cornstarch to make a thin paste. Add with tapioca to fruit mixture and cook for 10 minutes. Stir in sugar and cook for 2 minutes longer. Remove from heat and add lemon juice. Serve warm, with cream.

Makes 6 servings.

Barbara Clancey
Gloucester, Massachusetts

SWEDISH FRUIT SOUP

6 cups water
1 cup prunes
1 cup seedless raisins
1 stick cinnamon
1 cup diced apples
¼ cup sugar

3 tablespoons
  quick-cooking tapioca
1 package (10 ounces)
  frozen raspberries,
  thawed
Few drops of lime juice

☐Pour water over prunes and raisins and add cinnamon and apples. Cook until fruit is tender, then stir in sugar and tapioca and cook until thickened. Add raspberries and lime juice last.

Makes 6 to 8 servings.

Mrs. Ethel Salters
Weymouth, Massachusetts

COLD YOGURT SOUP

Be sure everything is *cold*, including the serving bowls. The small Oriental bowl is effective.

2 cups plain yogurt
¾ teaspoon salt and
  pepper
¼ teaspoon Tabasco
⅛ teaspoon dillweed
½ cup nuts of your
  choice, minced
1½ teaspoons chopped
  fresh chives

1 canned red pimiento
1 cup club soda
⅓ cup heavy cream,
  whipped
1 can (6½ ounces) tuna,
  lobster, crab, or shrimp,
  drained

☐ This is a great blender affair. Blend the yogurt, salt, pepper, Tabasco, dillweed, minced nuts, chives, and pimiento in the blender. Turn into bowl and add the club soda. Fold in the whipped cream just before serving, likewise the chosen seafood. Serve chilled.

Makes 4 servings.

Harriet C. Hughes
Jamaica Plain, Massachusetts

Dave's Note: Super dish. Don't tell people what's in it! (Some refused to try it because of the name.)

CANTALOUPE SOUP (COLD)

If you're not used to serving warm-weather soups, try this one for that unexpected touch with lunch or dinner. The subtle blending of these few ingredients makes the final result a refreshing treat, especially on a hot day. Be sure the soup is thoroughly chilled to bring out its unusual flavor.

1 large ripe cantaloupe
½ teaspoon ground
  cinnamon

2 tablespoons lime juice
2 cups orange juice
Fresh mint sprigs

☐Remove seeds from cantaloupe and cube the flesh. Purée flesh with the cinnamon in a blender or food processor. Combine lime juice and orange juice and stir into the purée. Chill and serve in chilled soup bowls. Garnish with mint sprigs.

Makes 6 servings.

Miss Priscilla E. McKay
Gloucester, Massachusetts

Dave's Note: Cool and colorful.

COLD PLUM SOUP

2 cans (17 ounces each)
   purple plums
⅓ cup lime juice
⅔ cup light rum

Ground cinnamon
Dash of ground cloves
Whipped cream (optional)

☐Drain plums, reserving liquid. Remove pits from plums. Combine plums, reserved liquid, lime juice, rum, ⅛ teaspoon cinnamon, and cloves in a large bowl, mixing together about a third at a time. Refrigerate covered for about 4 hours or overnight. (It may be placed in a freezer for 1 to 2 hours to chill more quickly.) Serve in chilled glasses garnished with a dab of whipped cream and sprinkled with cinnamon.

Makes 4 servings.

Sheila Martin
Massachusetts

CHILIS

☞ WHAT FOLLOWS is the results of the Dave Maynard Chili Contest or "The Day of the Almost Terminal Heartburn."

I love to do good contests. It's great to see lots of people win lots of nice prizes. When Delta Airlines asked me if I'd like to host a chili contest, I just naturally said yes. After all, first prize was an all-expense-paid weekend for two in Dallas with me as the chaperone. I'd never been to Big D, so I looked forward to the whole thing. Of course, I've served as a chaperone *many* times.

Then, I was told, "You have to be one of the judges and there will *only* be twenty-five finalists"! Twenty-five different chilis to sample? Spread out over how long? Oh, a couple of hours.

Now, let me tell you about me and beans. Oboy! Any beans— kidney, pea, navy, pinto, yellow eye, no difference. You can throw in chick-peas and lentils and, well, I guess you get the idea. David M. and legumes is a dangerous idea. If I had an isolation ward maybe things would be different, but I don't—and please remember, I have an image to protect (ho ho!).

Ah, what a day that was. Twenty-five humming crockpots at Guadalaharry's Restaurant in historic Quincy Marketplace. Three judges, and pitchers of cold white wine and margaritas at the ready. (By the way, that was my first introduction to this Mexican madness, and I truthfully felt at the end of the day that I would have the world's first talking liver.)

Well, to make it short, it was a super day! Talk about an era of good feeling! We started at about eleven or twelve and finished three hours later. It got pretty informal before it was over. I remember dancing with some of the contestants. Most of the women did okay, but the guys really tangoed lousy.

Anyway, Al Sims from Merrymeeting Lake, New Hampshire, won. He grew up in Oklahoma during the grapes-of-wrath years and learned that good chili was the staple of many a home. I imagine that, between the meat and the spices, there were a lot of happier stomachs. You'll notice the absence of beans in Al's prize-winning recipe. When I asked rather casually where they were, I got a pair of the highest eyebrows I've ever seen. Beans? Beans? Never! Hey Al, that's okay by me.

We had a great Dallas weekend. Being driven to the Fort Worth Stockyards to visit Billy Bob's, the world largest saloon. (I mean thirty-two bars all under one roof.) Every dude in the place dressed in jeans, plaid shirts, cowboy boots and one of them big hats you never take off unless you're daid, except for me. I had to wear a dark-blue, three-piece pin-striped suit. I got away with it, though—I just told everybody I was Conway Twitty.

Nice time, good contest. Great chilis, and here they are.

PRIZE-WINNING CHILI CON CARNE

10 pounds chuck roast
  (bone in), or 8 pounds
  deboned
1 cup vegetable oil
½ cup chili powder
¼ cup cumin powder
¼ cup salt
2 tablespoons black pepper
¼ tablespoon crushed
  red pepper
9 small hot peppers,
  chopped

6 large sweet red peppers,
  chopped
2 cans (35 ounces each)
  whole tomatoes,
  undrained
1 can (12 ounces) tomato
  paste
1 can (8 ounces) tomato
  sauce

☐Debone meat, if necessary, and cut away all excess fat; cut meat into ¼ to 1-inch cubes. Place meat in a 4-quart pressure cooker and add oil, chili powder, cumin powder, salt, black pepper, and crushed red pepper. Cook under pressure for one hour. (If you do not have a pressure cooker, use a roasting pan with cover and cook in a 350°F oven for several hours or until meat is stringy.)

Chop hot and sweet peppers. Put peppers and whole tomatoes with liquid into a 10-quart pot. Mix thoroughly and cook over low heat until meat is ready. Add meat and tomato paste and sauce. Bring to a boil, stirring frequently. Reduce to simmer, cover, and cook slowly for 2 to 3 hours, stirring frequently. If there's excess liquid, add a little cornmeal. You may also add 2 to 3 tablespoons of pinto beans if you wish.

Yields approximately 18 delicious cups.

Al Sims
Merrymeeting Lake, New Hampshire
But grew up in Oklahoma

REAL TEXAS CHILI

2 tablespoons vegetable oil
3 pounds boneless beef
   chuck, cut into 1-inch
   cubes
3 to 4 cloves garlic, minced
6 tablespoons chili powder
2 teaspoons ground cumin
3 tablespoons all-purpose
   flour

1 tablespoon dried oregano
2 cans (13¾ ounces each)
   beef broth
1 teaspoon salt
¼ teaspoon pepper
1 cup dairy sour cream
1 lime, cut into wedges

☐Heat oil in 4-quart kettle or heavy-bottomed pan over medium heat. Add beef, stirring frequently with a wooden spoon until meat changes color but does not brown. Lower heat and stir in garlic. Combine chili powder, cumin, and flour and sprinkle over meat, stirring until evenly coated. Sprinkle oregano over meat.

Add 1½ cans of the beef broth, stirring until liquid is well blended. Add salt and pepper and bring to a boil, stirring occasionally. Reduce heat.

Simmer, partially covered, for 1½ hours, stirring occasionally. Add remaining broth and cook for 30 minutes, or until meat is almost falling apart.

Cool thoroughly. Cover and refrigerate overnight to ripen flavor. Serve garnished with sour cream and a lime wedge to squeeze over each portion.

Makes 8 to 10 servings.

Linda W. Nichols
Melrose, Massachusetts

RHODE ISLAND RED

3 pounds sweet red peppers, seeded and chopped in ½-inch squares
3 pounds onions, coarsely chopped
1 can (28 ounces) tomato purée
1 can (10½ ounces) tomato soup
1 bottle (12 ounces) imported beer
2 ounces chili powder
1 tablespoon ground cumin
1 tablespoon dried basil
1 teaspoon dried parsley flakes
½ teaspoon crushed bay leaves
½ teaspoon salt
½ teaspoon pepper
Pinch of dried oregano
2 tablespoons cider vinegar
3 tablespoons sugar
½ teaspoon garlic powder
1 tablespoon Worcestershire sauce
1 small jalapeño pepper, chopped
Tomato paste
2 pounds ground beef
1 pound lean bacon, cooked and crumbled

☐ Combine all ingredients except tomato paste, beef, and bacon in a large pot. Bring to a boil, stirring often. Lower heat, cover, and simmer for 1 hour. Brown beef, then add to pot, along with cooked bacon, and simmer for 1 hour longer. Add tomato paste to thicken as desired.

Makes 8 servings.

Bill Hughes
N. Providence, Rhode Island

Best aged a day.

FRIJOLE FREDDY'S FIERY RIO RED

This recipe is the culmination of four years of intensive study under the tutelage of greater Dallas' most incendiary chili heads, my friends and neighbors. Living in "Big D" it was my pleasure to share authentic Lone Star potluck with some of the warmest and friendliest people it's ever been my pleasure to know. The variety, quality, and stand-up-and-be-counted-ness of this chili I owe to them. Anything you don't like (and for the life of me I can't understand what more anyone could ask for) you can blame on yours truly.

6 bacon slices, cut into ¼-inch strips
2 pounds ground beef round
2 pounds flank steak or mule-deer chuck, cut in ¼- to ½-inch dice
2 large onions, chopped
6 medium garlic cloves, finely chopped
6 large ripe tomatoes or 2 large jars home-canned whole tomatoes, chopped
6 bottles (12 ounces each) Mexican dark beer

1 tablespoon cider vinegar
1 tablespoon dried oregano, preferably Mexican
4 large green bell peppers, seeded and chopped
4 fresh jalepeño chilis or 1 small can
3 tablespoons ground cumin
2 pounds spicy sausage
3 tablespoons ground hot red chili
3 tablespoons ground mild red chili
3 tablespoons paprika
1 teaspoon black pepper

2 bunches fresh scallions
1½ pounds small pinto
   beans
1½ cups grated sharp
   cheddar cheese
   (optional)

2 whole green chili peppers
2 whole red chili peppers
2 cups tequila (optional)

☐Cook bacon strips in heavy iron skillet over medium heat. Add beef and steak cubes and sauté until light gray. Add onions and garlic and continue to sauté.

Place tomatoes in 10-quart pot and add 2 bottles of the beer, the vinegar, and meat mixture and bring to a boil. Reduce heat and simmer, covered, for 1 to 3 hours. Add oregano, bell peppers, jalepeños, and cumin and continue simmering. Cut up sausage and add to pot with all of the chili powder, paprika and black pepper. Add 2 more bottles of beer and continue simmering for 2 more hours. Remove pot from heat and let cool. Refrigerate overnight.

The following day, skim fat from top of pot. Add sliced scallions and return to heat to simmer. In a separate pot bring pinto beans to a boil with remaining 2 bottles of beer (add water if needed). Add beans to chili and simmer, covered, until beans are cooked to taste.

Top with cheddar cheese, if desired, and garnish with red and green chili peppers.

Option: Before adding garnish, add 2 cups of tequila and stir thoroughly.

Makes about 16 servings.

Fred Walczyck
Dallas, Texas

TEXAS CHILI

The only real spectacular remark I have to make is that each time I've had the pleasure of making this I've had the same compliments. I used the recipe for many years while my six children were growing up, and somewhere along the way someone told me that if I added 4 cups of shredded lettuce to it, it would give the chili an added zesty taste. It did.

1 pound ground beef	**1 teaspoon oregano**
1¼ cups chopped onion	**1 teaspoon pepper**
1 cup chopped green	**½ teaspoon salt**
pepper	**4 cups shredded lettuce**
2 cans (10½ ounces each)	**1 can (19 ounces) red**
beef broth	**kidney beans**
2 cans (8 ounces each)	**4 ounces sharp cheddar**
tomato sauce	**cheese, shredded**
2 tablespoons chili powder	

☐Brown meat in large heavy skillet. Drain off grease and add onion and peppers. Cook until tender. Stir in beef broth, tomato sauce, chili powder, and other seasonings. Simmer, uncovered, for 20 minutes. Remove skillet from heat. Combine lettuce and kidney beans and add to meat sauce. Toss lightly. Sprinkle with cheese and serve immediately.

Makes 8 servings.

Hazel A. Dyer
Troy, New Hampshire

JIM'S CHILI

The recipe "Jim's Chili" is the result of five years of obsessive, heartburning hours of cooking and testing over a large, black cast iron skillet. But I loved every minute of it, and believe it or not, my wife June survived every simmering bowl. There are now two versions of this recipe. The obsession continues!

The common denominator among chili eaters, with or without beans, with beer, wine or ice tea, is the romance of consuming the slowly cooked stew in the company of good friends. It is a food without season, good in the heat of the summer or the cold of the winter. The completion of a successful batch is occasion enough.

1 pound hot Italian sausage	1 tablespoon sugar
2 pounds lean ground beef	3 tablespoons chili powder
1 large white onion, diced	½ teaspoon crushed hot
1 large red onion, diced	red pepper
1 large green pepper,	¼ teaspoon nutmeg
seeded and diced	1 teaspoon ground
3 cloves garlic, minced	cinnamon
1 can (28 ounces) crushed	2½ teaspoons salt
tomatoes	½ teaspoon black pepper
1 can (28 ounces) whole	2 whole bay leaves
tomatoes	1 or 2 cans (16-ounce size)
1 can (6 ounces) tomato	red kidney beans or
paste	pinto beans
2 cups red wine	
2 teaspoons ground cumin	

☐In a large saucepan, brown sausage (broken up finely). Remove from pan with slotted spoon and brown beef. Place beef and sausage in a medium or large stew pot and add all of the remaining ingredients except the beans. Stir to blend, cover, and simmer for 3 hours, stirring often. Add beans and simmer, covered, for 1 hour longer, stirring often.

Remove bay leaves and serve with grated sharp cheddar cheese, chopped onion, and sour cream as toppings.

Makes 10 to 12 servings.

Jim Coates
South Lyndeboro, New Hampshire

CHOCOLATE CHILI CON CARNE

Seriously, folks, this chili tastes nothing like a candy bar or any other chocolate confection! I, too, was a bit skeptical when I first heard of the addition of chocolate to a simmering kettle of chili. But when I finally included the bittersweet chocolate in my tried and true chili recipe, everyone was impressed by the rich, dark color and subtle flavor in this new version of an old favorite. So try it—you'll like it, too!

2 pounds ground beef
1 cup chopped onion
¼ cup diced green
   pepper
2 large cloves garlic,
   minced
1 tablespoon vegetable oil
1 can (6 ounces) tomato
   paste

2 cans (16-ounce-size each)
   whole tomatoes,
   undrained
1 ounce bittersweet
   chocolate
¼ to ⅓ cup chili powder
1 teaspoon salt
2 cans (16 ounces each) red
   kidney beans, undrained

☐ In a 5-quart Dutch oven or large pot, sauté beef, onion, green pepper, and garlic in hot oil until onion is tender and beef loses its redness, stirring often. Add tomato paste, tomatoes with liquid, chocolate, chili powder, and salt. Bring to a boil. Reduce heat, cover, and simmer for 1 hour, stirring occasionally. Stir in beans with liquid and heat through.

Serve with toppings of shredded cheese and lettuce. If no fire extinguisher is available, substitute orange sherbet for dessert.

Makes 8 to 10 servings.

Pamela Finer
Malden, Massachusetts

MACHO MAN CHILI

My father is now a retired Army sergeant, but while he was in the service, he always brought home the troops for a home-cooked meal. Although this recipe is not one my mother used, it's one I used a lot when my husband, also in the service, brought home the guys for a home-cooked meal. It's been serviced all over Europe and the U.S.

2 pounds ground beef
1½ cups chopped onion
2 cloves garlic, finely
   chopped
1 cup chopped green
   pepper (optional)
1 can (28 ounces) whole
   tomatoes, undrained

2 cans (16 ounces each)
   whole kidney beans,
   undrained
2 teaspoons salt
2 tablespoons chili powder
1 teaspoon pepper
1 teaspoon ground cumin

☐ Brown ground beef in frying pan, along with onion, garlic, and green pepper. Place tomatoes with liquid, kidney beans with liquid, salt, chili powder, pepper, and cumin in crockpot or other slow cooker. Stir in beef mixture and cook on low setting for 5 to 8 hours.

Makes 8 to 10 servings.

Liv Hooper
Amesbury, Massachusetts

THREE BEAN CHILI

Doubling the recipe has been a wonderful way to serve my husband, Mac's, basketball teammates when the "Fraconia Stingers" met his team from the Pepperell-Groton-Lowell area.

1 pound ground beef
1 envelope Chili-O brand
   or other chili mix
1 can (16 ounces) green
   beans, undrained
1 can (16 ounces) wax
   beans, undrained

1 can (16 ounces) kidney
   beans, undrained
1 can (16 ounces) stewed
   tomatoes
1½ cups cooked macaroni

☐ Brown ground beef in a large skillet and add all other ingredients. Heat through.

Makes 8 servings.

Macbeth Reid
Pepperell, Massachusetts

MA BELLE'S CHILI

The name was given by my two daughter's friends all of whom call me Ma Belle. Whenever their friends came, which seemed every day, they always wanted "Ma Belle's chili." The basic recipe was my dear mother's; however, I being a semivegetarian, added any fresh vegetables that were around.

1 teaspoon salt
1 pound ground beef
4 cloves garlic, chopped
2 medium onions, chopped
½ cup chopped celery
1 green pepper, seeded and
  chopped
1 large carrot, pared and
  chopped
1 cup sliced fresh
  mushrooms

1 can (10½ ounces) tomato
  soup
1½ soup cans tomato juice
1 can (16 ounces) red
  kidney beans, undrained
1 tablespoon cayenne
  pepper
1 tablespoon crushed red
  pepper
Grated Romano cheese

☐ Sprinkle salt over bottom of heavy skillet. Brown beef, garlic, onions and celery together. Add other ingredients except the cheese, cover, and simmer for about 1 hour. Add extra tomato juice or water if too dry.

Top with grated Romano cheese when serving.
Makes 8 servings.

Mrs. Theodore Slifer
West Yarmouth, Massachusetts

FRANK 'N' CHILI MANICOTTI OLÉ

I am a hot dog and pasta lover and have, over the years, collected any recipe containing the above. When I found this recipe with both hot dogs and pasta, it blew my mind!

10 manicotti shells
10 hot dogs

6 ounces Monterey Jack
  cheese

| 2 cans (15 ounces each) | 1 can (7½ ounces) |
| chili with beans | tomatoes with jalapeños |

☐Cook manicotti according to package directions. Drain and set aside. Broil hot dogs until some fat has cooked out. Shred two-thirds of cheese and set aside; cut remaining cheese into 4-inch strips. Split hot dogs lengthwise and insert a strip of cheese in each; place one cheese-stuffed hotdog inside each cooked manicotti shell. In medium-size bowl, combine chili with beans and tomatoes with jalapeños.

Preheat oven to 350°F.

Spoon about 2 cups of mixture into bottom of 13×9×2-inch baking dish. Arrange the manicotti shells on top, pouring remaining chili mixture over them. Cover and bake for 25 minutes. Uncover, sprinkle shredded cheese on top, and bake for 10 more minutes, or until cheese is melted and mixture is heated through.

Makes 5 or 6 servings.

Lillian Barry
Marblehead, Massachusetts

MORNING-AFTER CHILI

I am the only member of my 100 percent Italian family who enjoys really hot foods. I put red pepper on everything—even breakfast foods! So naturally when I first had chili at a Mexican restaurant, I fell in love with it. After trying a very basic recipe that I got from a local newspaper, and being very disappointed with it, I began adding—first *much* more red pepper (very hot) and then other ingredients I thought would "jazz" it up, while not going too far—the overall flavor was the important thing.

The only problem remaining was that nobody else—friends or relatives—would eat the chili as hot as I liked to make it. That's why, from now on, I usually make two batches when I cook it. One is hot and the other is *hotter*.

I've always loved to cook—my grandfather was a head chef at Worcester's old Sheraton Hotel (long since gone), and I guess I picked up the love of cooking from him. Another thing I picked up from him was a love of gardening. So, as soon as chili cooking became a preoccupation with me, an interest in Mexican spices and peppers naturally followed. I started growing and putting up many varieties of hot peppers, jalapeños being my favorite (they are also the hottest). These greatly enhanced my chili recipe.

10 ounces dried pinto beans
1½ pounds boneless lean beef
1½ pounds boneless pork
2 large onions, chopped
6 cloves garlic, crushed
1 can (4 ounces) crushed tomatoes
1 teaspoon salt
6 tablespoons olive oil
1 bay leaf
1¾ tablespoons ground cumin
6 teaspoons hot chili powder
2 to 3 teaspoons chili caribe

3 dried cayenne peppers, crushed
1 teaspoon dried oregano
½ teaspoon capers
¼ cup raisins
¼ to ½ cup plain brandy
½ teaspoon blackstrap molasses
2 to 3 teaspoons unsweetened cocoa powder
2 tablespoons masa harina (corn flour) to thicken, if desired
2 to 3 jalapeño peppers, diced
½ cup natural creamy peanut butter

☐Soak dried beans overnight in cold water.

Coarse grind half of meat and cut rest into ½-inch cubes. In 5-quart Dutch oven, sauté onion and garlic in hot olive oil. Remove from pot. Brown meat in same oil. Return onion and garlic to pot. Add remaining ingredients, except peanut butter and beans, to pot. Simmer, uncovered, for 2 hours, stirring often and adding water as needed. Stir in peanut butter and cook another 3 hours, still stirring and adding water often. In a separate pot cook beans for 1 hour in enough water to cover by an inch. Drain and add beans to chili. Cook for 10 minutes more.

Makes about 12 servings.

Bob Rossetti
Holden, Massachusetts

CHILI CON JOLIE

It doesn't have to be old to be good! (Ask Dave!) My "Chili Con Jolie" was a spur-of-the-moment invention. I had never made chili in my life but took the challenge. After much taste-testing by my relatives and neighbors, I bought shares in Alka-Seltzer and submitted my concoction.

Violà—a winner is born and heartburn lives on!

4 slices bacon
8 small Italian sausage
   links, sliced
1 pound boneless beef stew
   meat, cut in cubes
1 small green pepper,
   chopped
1 cup chopped scallion
1 clove garlic, minced
2 pickled jalapeño peppers,
   seeded and chopped
1 tablespoon chili powder
½ teaspoon crushed red
   pepper
½ teaspoon salt

¼ teaspoon dried
   oregano
2½ cups water
1 tablespoon tequila
1 tablespoon brown sugar
1 can (12 ounces) tomato
   paste
1 teaspoon instant beef
   bouillon
1 bay leaf
1 can (16 ounces) pinto
   beans
1 cup pimiento-stuffed
   olives
Avocados (optional)

☐Sprinkle bacon lightly with flour and cook until crisp in large saucepan. Drain and crumble; set aside. Brown sausage in same pan, remove, and set aside, leaving 2 tablespoons drippings in skillet. Brown diced beef, scallions, green pepper, and garlic in drippings. Add bacon, sausage, jalapeño peppers, chili powder, crushed red pepper, salt, and oregano. Stir in water, tequila, bouillon granules, brown sugar, and tomato paste. Bring to a boil. Add bay leaf and reduce heat. Simmer, uncovered, for 1½ hours, stirring occasionally. Add drained pinto beans and olives. Simmer, covered, for 30 minutes more. May be served in peeled seeded avocado halves.

Makes 8 servings.

Sue Jolie
Sturbridge, Massachusetts

THE NORTH DAKOTA SPECIAL

This chili is a *meal* chili; eat one or two bowls without regretting it later. I've made this chili for ten years, and it comes out great every time. Originally I'm from North Dakota and have enjoyed eating deer meat cooked in different ways. Adding deer meat to my chili lends it a distinct taste and reminds me of my days back home; if it is not available, use ground beef instead. Serve with saltine crackers or bread.

2 pounds ground beef
1 pound ground venison (mixed with ground pork)
1 can (12 ounces) stewed tomatoes
1 can (16 ounces) whole tomatoes, undrained
1 sweet green pepper, seeded and chopped
3 medium onions, coarsely chopped
6 small to medium cloves garlic, chopped
1 can (4 ounces) green chilis, chopped
4 stalks celery, diced

1½ cups water
2 cans (16 ounces each) red kidney beans, drained
1 squirt garlic juice
2 tablespoons chili powder
1 tablespoon ground cumin
1 teaspoon freshly ground pepper
1 teaspoon dried basil
1 bay leaf
Pinch of Italian seasoning
1 teaspoon salt
3 or 4 dashes Tabasco
10 ounces fresh mushrooms, sliced
1 cup semidry red wine
1 tablespoon brown sugar

☐Brown ground beef in frying pan at low heat; brown deer-burger in chili pot at low heat. Drain off grease and add beef to chili pot. Add stewed tomatoes and whole tomatoes, chopped, with juice. Add sweet green pepper, onions, garlic, chilis, celery and water. Simmer and stir. Add drained kidney beans, garlic juice, spices, herbs, salt, and Tabasco. Add mushrooms, wine, and sugar to pot. Stir and simmer for 1½ to 2 hours, covered. Add additional spices to taste before serving.

Makes about 12 servings.

Joseph C. Moser
North Weymouth, Massachusetts

MARIE'S DIET CHILI

Deliciously low in calories but hot and spicy.

1 pound ground turkey
2 tablespoons vegetable oil
1 large red onion, chopped
2 stalks celery, chopped
2 green peppers, chopped
1 can (16 ounces)
  French-style green
  beans
1 can (4 ounces) mushroom
  stems and pieces

3 cups tomato juice
½ teaspoon ground
  cumin
½ teaspoon garlic
  powder
1 package Sweet 'n' Low
3 tablespoons chili powder

☐Brown turkey in hot oil and drain off all fat. Place turkey in a medium-size pot and add all of the other ingredients. Stir well and cook, uncovered, for 45 minutes, or until very thick.

Makes 4 servings.

Maria Macchione
Revere, Massachusetts

UPSIDE-DOWN CHILI PIE

1½ pounds ground beef
  chuck
½ cup chopped onion
1 clove garlic, crushed
1 tablespoon vegetable oil
1 tablespoon chili powder
1¼ teaspoons salt
1 teaspoon dried oregano
1 teaspoon dried basil
1 can (8¼ ounces) whole
  tomatoes, undrained
½ cup red wine

1 can (8½ ounces) kidney
  beans, undrained
1 package (12 ounces) corn
  muffin mix
1 can (8¾ ounces)
  cream-style corn
1 egg
½ cup milk
¼ cup grated cheddar
  cheese
Chopped fresh parsley

☐Sauté beef, onion, and garlic in hot oil in heavy 10-inch skillet until beef is browned, about 5 minutes. Add chili powder, salt, oregano, basil and tomatoes with liquid. Mix well and cook, covered, over low flame for 30 minutes. Stir in kidney beans with liquid and wine and cook for 10 minutes longer.

Preheat oven to 400°F.

Combine muffin mix, corn, egg, and milk in medium bowl; mix until moist. Skim fat from meat; spread muffin mixture evenly over meat. Bake for 25 minutes, or until top is golden brown. Let cool in skillet for 2 minutes, then invert skillet onto platter. Garnish with cheese and parsley.

Makes 8 servings.

Mrs. Shirley Slagle
Kingston, Massachusetts

SKYLINE CHILI

2 pounds ground beef
1 Bermuda onion, chopped
1 package onion soup mix

2 cloves garlic, crushed
1 can (15 ounces) tomato
  sauce

¼ cup chili powder
1 teaspoon ground
  cinnamon
½ teaspoon crushed red
  pepper
1 teaspoon Worcestershire
  sauce

4 cups water
½ teaspoon salt
½ teaspoon black pepper
Spice bag (5 bay leaves and
  30 whole allspice)
Grated Longhorn Colby
  cheese

☐ Brown beef with onion, soup mix, and garlic in large heavy skillet or pot. Add remaining ingredients, including spice bag but excepting the cheese, and simmer over medium heat for 3 hours, stirring occasionally. Remove spice bag before serving. When serving, top with the grated cheese.

Makes 8 servings.

Mary Megan Coughlan
Waltham, Massachusetts

LENTIL AND RICE CHILI

1 cup dried lentils
1¼ cups water
Salt
½ cup long-grain rice
3 tablespoons vegetable oil
1 cup chopped onion
1 cup chopped green
  pepper
1 clove garlic, minced

1 cup drained, chopped,
  peeled tomatoes
2 teaspoons chili powder
½ teaspoon dried
  oregano
½ teaspoon ground
  cumin
⅛ teaspoon black pepper

☐ Rinse lentils. Place in a large saucepan and add salt and enough cold water to cover lentils by about 2 inches. Bring to a boil. Reduce heat and simmer, covered, for 25 to 35 minutes, or until tender.

In a separate saucepan, bring 1¼ cups water and salt to boil. Add rice and simmer, covered, for 20 minutes. While lentils are

cooling, heat oil in a large heavy skillet. Add onion, green pepper, and garlic and sauté until tender. Stir in tomatoes, chili powder, oregano, cumin, ¼ teaspoon salt, and pepper to taste and remove from heat. Drain lentils, reserving liquid, and add lentils and rice to tomato mixture, using ½ cup of lentil liquid. Return to skillet and heat through.
Makes 4 servings.

Virginia Bleloch
West Somerville, Massachusetts

CHILI CON CARNE À LA LENTICCHI

This recipe originated in a small town in Italy—Riano, in the province of Aquila. My grandmother, Christina Bonitatibus Fantasia, a fabulous cook, taught it to my mother, Rosina Fantasia, who passed it on to me. Nutrition-wise, it deserves high points.

1½ cup dried kidney beans
1½ quarts water
½ pound dried lentils
2½ teaspoons salt
2 onions, chopped
1 green pepper, chopped
1 pound coarsely ground
  lean beef
2 tablespoons vegetable or
  olive oil

2 tablespoons butter
1 can (16 ounces) whole
  tomatoes
1 can (8 ounces) seasoned
  tomato sauce
2 tablespoons chili powder
2 bay leaves
½ teaspoon pepper
5 to 6 drops Tabasco sauce

☐Rinse kidney beans and place in pot with 1½ quarts of cold water and let stand overnight. Wash lentils and place in pot with enough water to cover. Cook over medium flame for 40 minutes. Set aside. Add 1 teaspoon of salt to beans and simmer, covered, until tender (follow package directions). Drain and reserve bean liquid. Sauté onion, green pepper, and meat in hot oil. Add 2 tablespoons butter and beans, tomatoes, tomato sauce, chili pow-

der, 1½ teaspoons salt, bay leaves, pepper, and Tabasco sauce. Cover and simmer for 1½ hours, adding reserved bean liquid if necessary. During the last half hour add cooked, drained lentils and stir well.
Serves 6.

Mrs. Elizabeth R. Gandolfo
W. Peabody, Massachusetts

NORTHWEST CHILI

1 can (14½ ounces) whole tomatoes
2 large onions
3 tablespoons vegetable oil
1 cup chopped green pepper
2 cloves garlic, minced or mashed
2 pounds ground turkey
2 cans (15 ounces each) kidney beans, drained
2 cans (15 ounces each) tomato sauce
¼ cup soy sauce
3 tablespoons chili powder
1 teaspoon ground cumin
1 teaspoon dried sage
1 teaspoon dried thyme
2 limes, cut into wedges
1 can (16 ounces) pinto beans, drained

☐Chop tomatoes and reserve juice; set aside. Chop onions and set aside ¾ cup. In a 6- to 8-quart pan over medium-high heat, heat oil; add remaining onion, green pepper, and garlic; sauté until onion is limp, stirring often. Shape turkey into bite-size pieces and add to pan. Cook over high heat until drippings begin to brown, stirring gently. Add tomatoes and juice, beans, tomato sauce, soy sauce, chili powder, cumin, sage, and thyme. Stir to free browned bits at bottom of pan. Transfer to a slow cooker and simmer on low heat for approximately 30 to 45 minutes. Pour into a bowl and top with reserved onion and lime wedges.
Makes 6 to 8 servings.

Dave's

Dave's Note: This is my own chili, not entered in the competition.

CASSEROLES

☞ WHEN I started cooking, at the age of ten, I realized quickly what many cooks know, that casseroles are designed basically for one purpose—to put a lot of different foods, which are at least hopefully compatible, into a dish and come up with something delicious. After all, it stands to reason, if you begin with lots of good things and blend them together, you really should end up with something sensational. However, people seem to regard the one-dish meal as something second rate—until they taste it. I think everyone would agree that great casseroles are an end result of the tremendous amount of thought that kitchen folk through the ages have used to mix inferior meats and vegetables together with herbs and seasonings and "secret ingredients," producing a hearty, fantastic, nutritional dish that everyone at the table can eye with glee and smack their lips in anticipation over.

When I was small, my mother used to take me to movie matinees. You think *you* remember back? I remember being taken to the ladies' room at intermission. I used to flatten myself against the opposite wall and take a slightly astounded delight in seeing all of the ladies' bloomers around their ankles. As I think back, it seems pretty funny, but then—wow—it was scary. Well, anyway, I noticed after many Bette Davis, Miriam Hopkins, Norma Shearer, and Barbara Stanwyck movies that they always served meat and potato meals. Isn't that funny? I never *even understood what* they were eating from all those dishes, because my mother always served from one big bowl. I knew then, my mother was right and *they* were wrong, because they never seemed to eat much and we ate like wolves. Do you know I never even realized we were poor?

My sister, Jean, gave me my first easy casserole recipe:

1. 1 pound hamburger
2. 1 can Campbell's Vegetable Soup
3. A sprinkle of bread crumbs

It tasted pretty good and it sure was easy.

RULE #1 for casserole cookers: Keep your mouth shut. Never tell *anybody* what's in it, where you got it, or how much it cost.

RULE #2. Use leftovers, of course, *but* be sure to include some fresh ingredients for texture, eye appeal, and contrast.

Let's face it, the casserole is the answer to *everybody*'s prayer, because

1. It's usually inexpensive
2. It's easy to prepare in advance
3. You can knock down at least two drinks while cooking
4. It's easy to serve hot
5. It can be (in most cases) refrozen
6. It can be given the most exotic or mysterious names
7. It's almost foolproof
8. It looks nice (don't forget the parsley or paprika or the croutons)

Please peruse the pleasant possibilities of the following casserole recipes. Some are an absolute snap, some are a trifle involved, but *all* have one thing in common; you can make them as they are, *or* you can venture into your own cooking confidence.

I have a very difficult time when I casserole. I don't stick to a recipe, and I don't remember where I wasn't true to it. However, I've tried to remember some of my favorites.

PERUGUARY PIE

This is a friendship recipe. It was passed down from an aunt to her niece, then along to two sisters-in-law. It was given to me by one of them. The only funny incident that I know of was when someone substituted lettuce for cabbage. The pie still tasted okay, but it did lose something in the translation.

Pie pastry for a 2-crust pie	1 envelope brown gravy
1 large onion, chopped	mix
(about 1 cup)	1 teaspoon salt
3 carrots, pared and	½ teaspoon pepper
chopped	2 teaspoons chopped fresh
2½ cups chopped cabbage	parsley
1 pound ground beef	1 cup hot water
2 tablespoons butter	1 egg, beaten

☐Preheat oven to 400°F.

Sauté the onion, carrots, cabbage, and beef in hot butter. Add gravy mix, salt, pepper, parsley, and hot water; simmer, uncovered for 5 minutes. Roll out half of pie pastry and fit it into a pie dish. Put beef mixture in the pie shell and cover top with the rolled-out top crust. Brush with beaten egg, then bake for 30 minutes.

Makes 6 to 8 servings.

Martha Chisam
Brockton, Massachusetts

VEAL SURPRISE CASSEROLE

I am a cookbook nut, and being born in London and brought up in the U.S.A., I found this in a super British cookbook. Britain has a name for producing poor cooks. This recipe will prove different, I trust.

2 pounds boneless stewing
   veal
2 tablespoons all-purpose
   flour
Salt and pepper
2 tablespoons butter
2 tablespoons olive oil
1 clove garlic, finely
   chopped

⅓ cup tomato purée
1 beef bouillon cube
2 cups boiling water
1 bay leaf
Pinch of dried thyme
Pinch of dried marjoram
12 black olives, pitted
¼ pound fresh
   mushrooms, sliced

☐Preheat oven to 350°F. Cut veal into cubes and dip in flour seasoned with salt and pepper. Brown veal cubes in butter and olive oil, together with the finely chopped garlic. Add tomato purée and bouillon cube dissolved in the boiling water. Add the herbs and seasonings. Bake, covered, for 1½ hours. Half an hour before casserole is finished, add pitted olives and sliced mushrooms.

Serve with fluffy white rice, garnished with stuffed olives and glazed onions. To make the glazed onions, saute 12 onions in butter in a saucepan with a lid on, shaking often. Meanwhile, cook 2 tablespoons packed brown sugar with 2 tablespoons vinegar in a small saucepan until a thick syrup is obtained. When the onions are cooked, put them in the syrup and boil for a few minutes, until they are well cooked.

Makes 6 servings.

Kathleen I. Burgess
Danvers, Massachusetts

CASSEROLE OF TONGUE

Years ago, an elderly friend of mine gave me this recipe. At first, my husband and daughter objected to eating tongue, but it turned out to be one of their favorite dishes.

1 beef tongue
2 tablespoons all-purpose
   flour

2 teaspoons cooking fat
1 teaspoon salt
¼ teaspoon pepper

1 cup sliced pared carrot

1 cup diced pared turnip

1 cup cooked peas

1 cup sliced celery

1 teaspoon minced onion

☐Wash tongue and simmer slowly until tender, approximately 1½ to 2 hours. Remove skin and trim. Place in a casserole. Preheat oven to 400°F. Combine flour, cooking fat, and 2 cups of broth from tongue. Add salt and pepper. Arrange vegetables around tongue; pour over sauce made with broth. Bake until vegetables are tender.

Makes 8 servings.

Alice Shepard
West Bridgewater, Massachusetts

NANA'S STUFFED STEAK CREOLE

1 cup bread crumbs

¼ cup chopped celery

2 medium onions, chopped

1 teaspoon chopped fresh parsley

1 beef round steak (about 2 pounds)

Salt and pepper to taste

Dried sage to taste

1 teaspoon butter, melted

1 can (16 ounces) crushed tomatoes

1 green pepper, seeded and chopped

Potatoes (as many as desired), peeled

☐Preheat oven to 350°F.

Mix together bread crumbs, half of chopped onions, the celery, and parsley. Spread, about 1 inch thick, over steak. Season with salt, pepper, and sage and drizzle melted butter over it. Roll steak and tie with a string; place in a large, deep pan. Mix tomatoes, remaining onion, and the green pepper in a bowl; pour on top of steak. Bake, uncovered, for 2 hours. Arrange peeled potatoes around meat and continue to bake for 1 more hour.

Makes 8 servings.

Mary York
Newbury, Massachusetts

CONNECTICUT BEEF SUPPER

2 large onions, thinly sliced
2 tablespoons cooking fat
   or butter
2 pounds boneless beef
   chuck, cut in 1-inch
   cubes
1 cup water
2 large potatoes, pared and
   sliced ⅛ inch thick
1 can (10½ ounces) cream
   of mushroom soup

1 cup sour cream
1¼ cups milk
1 teaspoon salt
¼ teaspoon pepper
1 cup grated cheddar
   cheese
½ cup crushed Wheaties
   (1¼ cups uncrushed)

☐Sauté onions in fat in a large saucepan. Add meat and water and cover. Reduce heat and simmer for 50 minutes.
Heat oven to 350°F.
Transfer meat to a 13×9-inch baking pan. Place sliced potatoes over meat. Blend soup, sour cream, milk, salt, and pepper and pour evenly over top. Sprinkle with cheese and Wheaties. Bake, uncovered, for 1½ hours, or until done.
Makes 6 to 8 servings.

Mrs. John Duggan
Falls Church, Virginia

ITALIENNE CASSEROLE

This recipe has been around our family for many years. Until recently, however, it was buried in a drawerful of well-worn cookbooks and yellowed recipe clippings from the newspaper. Needless to say, it was a pleasant surprise to find this long-lost recipe. A delicious variation of this casserole is to add a few sliced sweet Italian sausages. (Fry them first.) This filling casserole, served with fresh, hot garlic bread and a salad, makes a hearty, satisfying meal. It can easily be frozen.

2 pounds ground beef
2 medium onions, chopped
1 clove garlic, crushed
1 jar (14 ounces) spaghetti
  sauce
1 can (16 ounces) stewed
  tomatoes
1 jar (3 ounces) mushrooms

8 ounces cooked macaroni
  shells
2 cups sour cream
1½ pounds provolone
  cheese
½ pound mozzarella
  cheese

☐Brown ground beef, onions, and garlic in a large, heavy skillet. Combine spaghetti sauce, tomatoes, and mushrooms and add to beef. Simmer, uncovered, for 20 minutes.

Preheat oven to 350°F.

Put half the cooked shells in a casserole dish and cover with half of the meat sauce. Spread with half the sour cream and all of the provolone cheese. Repeat with remaining macaroni, meat sauce and sour cream; top with all of the mozzarella. Cover and bake for 35 minutes. Remove cover and bake for 10 to 15 minutes longer to brown.

Makes 8 servings.

Roselle Delsignore
Raynham, Massachusetts

MEXICAN CORNBREAD CASSEROLE

1 pound ground beef
½ cup chopped onions
⅓ cup chopped green
  pepper
1½ teaspoons chili powder
1 clove garlic, minced
1 can (6 ounces) tomato
  paste
¼ cup water
1 egg
1 package (3 ounces) cream
  cheese

1 can (8 ounces)
  cream-style corn
½ cup shredded cheddar
  cheese
½ cup yellow cornmeal
½ cup all-purpose flour
2 teaspoons baking powder
⅓ cup milk
2 tablespoons butter,
  melted
Dash of Tabasco

☐Preheat oven to 400°F. In a skillet, brown beef, onion, green pepper, chili powder, and garlic; drain off fat. Add tomato paste mixed with ¼ cup water. Spread into a 2-quart oblong baking dish or a 9-inch-square pan. In a small bowl blend cream cheese and egg until smooth; stir in corn. Spoon this mixture over beef and sprinkle with cheddar cheese.

To make cornbread, combine cornmeal, flour, baking powder, and salt. Stir in milk blended with remaining egg, butter, and Tabasco, just until dry ingredients are moistened. Spoon onto meat-corn mixture and spread gently. Bake for 30 minutes or until top is golden brown.

Carrie Phelps
Hillsboro, New Hampshire

Dave's Note: I added a little more chili powder.

BAKED KIBBEE

2 cups medium cracked
  wheat
2 pounds ground lean lamb
  or half ground lamb
  and half ground beef
1 large onion, chopped

¼ cup pine nuts,
  coarsely ground
½ teaspoon ground
  cinnamon
Salt and pepper to taste

☐Soak wheat in water to cover for 30 minutes. Drain, then mix with half of the meat, the onion, and salt and pepper to taste. Make a filling consisting of remaining meat, the pine nuts, cinnamon, and more salt and pepper to taste. Brown filling in a skillet.

Preheat oven to 450°F. Butter a 14 × 10-inch baking pan.

Divide wheat-meat (kibbee) mixture in half. Spread half in bottom of pan. Spread filling next and then top with remaining half of the kibbee mixture. Moisten hands and smooth top layer, then cut top into diamond shapes. Bake for 30 to 40 minutes.

Makes 8 servings.

Anne Depoian
Chelmsford, Massachusetts

MONTEZUMA PIE

2 tablespoons vegetable oil
1 onion, finely chopped
2 pounds ground beef
1 can (10 ounces) enchilada
  sauce
1 can (8 ounces) tomato
  sauce
1 cup canned corn kernels,
  drained
2 teaspoons salt

½ teaspoon freshly
  ground pepper
¼ teaspoon dried
  rosemary, crumbled
¼ teaspoon dried
  oregano, crumbled
12 flour tortillas
3 cups grated sharp
  cheddar cheese

☐Heat oil in a large skillet over medium-high heat. Add onion
and sauté until softened, about 3 to 5 minutes. Add beef and cook
until browned, stirring frequently. Drain off any excess fat. Combine enchilada and tomato sauces in a small bowl. Pour half into
meat mixture. Blend in corn, salt, pepper, rosemary, and oregano
and bring to a boil. Reduce heat and simmer, uncovered, for 5
minutes.

Preheat oven to 350°F. Grease a 13×9-inch baking dish.

Arrange 6 tortillas in bottom of prepared dish. Add meat mixture, spreading evenly. Sprinkle with half of cheese. Arrange
remaining tortillas over top. Cover with remaining sauce and
sprinkle with remaining cheese. Cover with foil and bake until
heated through, about 15 to 20 minutes. Serve immediately.

Makes 8 to 10 servings.

Dave's

CHILIED RIBS

4 to 5 pounds lean beef
  short ribs, cut into 2- to
  3-inch lengths
1 large onion, cut in pieces
¼ cup finely chopped
  canned hot chilies

2 cloves garlic, minced
1 cup catsup or tomato-
  based chili sauce
1 cup water
1 tablespoon dry mustard
1 tablespoon vinegar

2 tablespoons (packed)   3 cups hot, cooked rice
    brown sugar   Fresh coriander or parsley

☐Preheat oven to 425°F. Place ribs in a 4- to 5-quart casserole and arrange onion pieces around the meat. Stir half the chilies with all the garlic, catsup, water, mustard, sugar, and vinegar, then pour over meat.

Cover tightly and bake until meat is very tender when pierced and pulls easily from the bone, about 2½ hours. Stir several times. To serve, lift meat from pan and place on a serving platter. Remove fat from juice and heat to boil, then add remaining chilis. You should have about ¾ cup. Spoon rice on platter with ribs, and pour meat juices over all. Garnish with coriander.

Makes 4 to 6 servings.

Dave's

HAM AND CABBAGE CASSEROLE

¼ cup butter or   ¼ cup chopped green
    margarine   pepper
¼ cup flour   1¼ pounds cabbage,
2 cups milk   coarsely shredded
¾ cup shredded   1½ cups buttered bread
    American cheese   crumbs
1 pound cooked ham, diced

☐Preheat oven to 350°F.

Melt butter in saucepan over low heat. Slowly stir in flour until smooth. Add milk, stirring constantly. Cook until thickened. Add cheese, ham, and green pepper to sauce. Meanwhile, boil cabbage in water for 5 minutes and drain.

In a buttered 3-quart casserole dish, place a layer of cabbage, then a layer of ham and cheese sauce. Repeat. Sprinkle buttered crumbs on top. Bake for 30 minutes.

Makes 6 to 8 servings.

Mrs. Nina Pilla
Waltham, Massachusetts

VICKI'S SAUERKRAUT MEATBALL CASSEROLE

This recipe is much simpler to prepare than it may appear. It requires very little attention while baking and cannot be over-cooked. It is a good, hot, satisfying dish and has less cholesterol than the conventional "sauerkraut and pork"; it is very good served with a light, fluffy dumpling. Leftovers are even better (if you have any left over!).

1½ pounds ground lean beef
¾ cup rice
1 teaspoon finely chopped onion
1 egg
Salt and pepper to taste
Paprika to taste

1 large can sauerkraut, undrained
1 cup coarsely shredded cabbage
1 apple, peeled, cored, and shredded
1 teaspoon brown sugar

☐Preheat oven to 350°F.

Mix together ground beef, rice, onion, egg, and salt, pepper, and paprika to taste. Form into balls about twice the size of a walnut. Place cabbage in a large casserole and top with sauer-kraut, including the juice, and apple. Place meatballs over top of kraut mixture and sprinkle with brown sugar. Cover with a lid or foil and bake for 1 hour or longer. Add more water as needed, as it is absorbed by the rice in the baking process. Remove lid and bake for about 30 minutes longer, until meatballs become a light, toasty brown.

Makes 6 to 8 servings.

Vicki E. Sharpe
Johnstown, Pennsylvania

CORNED BEEF IN CASSEROLE

6 tablespoons butter
2 onions, finely chopped
1 clove garlic, finely
   chopped
1 green pepper, seeded and
   cut into thin strips
2 cans (15 ounces each)
   corned beef hash

1 teaspoon dry mustard
1 tablespoon
   Worcestershire sauce
6 tablespoons chopped
   fresh parsley
Buttered bread crumbs
Grated cheese (Parmesan,
   Swiss, or cheddar)

☐Preheat oven to 400°F.

Melt butter in a skillet and sauté the onions, garlic, and green pepper until soft. Add corned beef hash, dry mustard, and Worcestershire sauce. Place half of hash mixture in a buttered casserole dish. Sprinkle with parsley and top with remaining hash. Top with buttered crumbs and grated cheese. Bake for 25 to 30 minutes, until brown.

Makes 6 servings.

Elizabeth Wessa
Brockton, Massachusetts

REUBEN CASSEROLE

This recipe doesn't have much of a history; we are sailors, and one-pot meals are a must, especially when we are on a trip. So one windy day at Block Island these wonderful smells invaded our boat, and the galley slave on the next boat gave me the recipe. With the exception of the cheese, you can use canned ingredients, but, of course, fresh sauerkraut and tomatoes taste better. A salad and a good imported beer go well with it.

1 pound sauerkraut, rinsed
    and drained
1 can (12 ounces) corned
    beef, or ¾ pound fresh
2½ cups shredded Swiss
    cheese
½ cup Thousand Island
    dressing

½ cup mayonnaise
2 tomatoes, peeled and
    thinly sliced
½ cup rye bread crumbs,
    toasted
2 tablespoons butter,
    melted

☐Preheat oven to 350°F.

Arrange sauerkraut in bottom of a 1½-quart glass or ceramic baking dish. Slice corned beef; layer it and cheese over sauerkraut. Combine salad dressing and mayonnaise in a small bowl. Spread evenly over cheese. Cover with tomato slices. Toss bread crumbs in melted butter and sprinkle over top of casserole. Bake until heated through and bubbly, about 30 to 40 minutes. Serve immediately.

Makes 4 to 6 servings.

Irmgard Hayes
Stafford, Vermont

HAM AND CHEESE DELIGHT

½ cup finely chopped
    onion
1 tablespoon butter or
    margarine
2 cups finely chopped ham
1 cup shredded processed
    sharp American cheese

1½ cups milk
3 eggs, beaten
⅔ cup finely crushed
    crackers (about 15)
Pinch of pepper

☐Preheat oven to 350°F. Sauté onion in butter or margarine until tender but not browned. Combine with all of the remaining ingredients and mix well. Pour into a greased 10 × 6 × 1½-inch baking dish. Bake for 45 to 50 minutes, or until a knife inserted in the center of the casserole comes out clean.

Makes 6 to 8 servings.

Lucille Townsend
Columbus, Indiana

HAM CASSEROLE

8 tablespoons butter or
    margarine
6 tablespoons and 1
    teaspoon flour
1½ cups milk
1½ cups light cream
1½ teaspoons salt
1½ teaspoons white pepper

¼ pound sharp cheddar
    cheese, grated
1 cup sliced mushrooms
1 medium onion, minced
1½ to 2 pounds baked
    ham, cubed
Buttered bread crumbs

☐Preheat oven to 350°F.

Melt 6 tablespoons of butter in a saucepan over low heat. Slowly add 6 tablespoons of flour, stirring constantly to make a smooth paste. Add milk and cream, gradually, stirring constantly until thickened. Season with salt and pepper. Add cheese and stir until melted. In a separate pan sauté mushrooms and onion in 2 tablespoons butter. Sprinkle with 1 teaspoon flour and add mixture to the cream sauce. Stir in ham and pour into a casserole dish. Bake for 30 to 45 minutes until bubbly and brown.

Esther M. Samson
Lexington, Massachusetts

SHANGHAI ONE-DISH

¼ cup vegetable oil
1 pound ground pork
2 cups chopped cabbage
1 large onion, chopped
1 large carrot, pared and
  shredded
5 ounces green beans,
  French-cut and sliced
  diagonally
3 or 4 medium dried black
  mushrooms, soaked in
  hot water 30 minutes,
  well drained and minced

1 teaspoon minced fresh
  ginger or ½ teaspoon
  ground ginger
¼ cup soy sauce, or to
  taste
1½ cups rice
2 cups chicken broth
2 small zucchini, unpeeled,
  shredded
Salt and freshly ground
  pepper
Minced green onion

☐ Heat oil in a wok over medium-high heat. Add pork and stir until meat loses pink color. Stir in cabbage, onion, carrot, beans, mushrooms, and ginger and stir-fry for two minutes. Mix in ¼ cup soy sauce. Add rice and stir gently. Pour in broth. Cover tightly and simmer until liquid is almost absorbed, about 20 to 25 minutes. Stir in zucchini and cook about 5 minutes longer. Season with salt and pepper and more soy sauce, if desired. Garnish with green onion and serve immediately.

Makes 8 servings.

Dave's

Dave's Note: Substitute beef if pork is not available.

PIZZA POT PIE

1½ pounds mild Italian
  sausage, casings
  removed
3 cloves garlic, minced or
  pressed

1 teaspoon fennel seed
1 teaspoon dried oregano
½ teaspoon pepper
3 ripe plum tomatoes,
  seeded and chopped

2 cups (about ½ pound)
  shredded mozzarella
  cheese
3 eggs, lightly beaten
¾ cup grated Parmesan
  cheese
¼ pound prosciutto, very
  thinly sliced

2 cups (about 1 pound)
  ricotta cheese
12 to 15 large fresh basil
  leaves
Pastry for a 2-crust
  12 × 8-inch pie

☐Crumble sausage in a 10- to 12-inch frying pan over medium heat. Cook, stirring, until meat is no longer pink, about 10 minutes. Add garlic, fennel seed, oregano, pepper, and tomato. Stir until mixture boils, about 5 minutes. Remove from heat and mix in mozzarella, lightly beaten eggs, and ½ cup of the Parmesan cheese. Set aside to cool slightly.

Preheat oven to 375°F.

On a lightly floured board, roll half of the pie pastry into an oval large enough to cover bottom and sides of an 12 × 8-inch oval baking dish. Fit pastry into dish, with excess lapped over rim.

Spoon sausage mixture evenly into crust and cover with prosciutto. Dot ricotta over prosciutto, then spread ricotta into even layer and top with basil leaves.

Roll remaining pastry out on a floured board until large enough to cover top of pie. Fit pastry over filling, seal edges, and flute. Pierce a few decorative holes in crust. Bake in a 375° oven until edge of crust is browned, about 1 hour. About 10 minutes before pie is done, sprinkle top with remaining Parmesan. Serve hot or at room temperature.

Makes 8 to 10 servings.

Dave's

BREAKFAST SOUFFLÉ

1½ pounds bulk pork
  sausage, crumbled
9 eggs, lightly beaten

3 cups milk
1½ teaspoons prepared
  mustard

1 teaspoon salt
1½ cups grated cheddar
cheese

3 slices white bread, cut in
¼-inch cubes

☐Brown crumbled sausage; drain well. In a large bowl, combine eggs, milk, mustard, and salt. Stir in bread, sausage and cheese. Pour into a greased 13×9-inch baking dish. Refrigerate, covered, overnight.
Preheat oven to 350°F.
Bake casserole, uncovered, for 1 hour.
Makes 12 servings.

Mrs. Jeannette Wicherts
Sterling, Illinois

SAUSAGE PILAF

1 pound bulk pork sausage
1 cup chopped celery
½ cup chopped onion
½ cup chopped green
pepper
¼ cup chopped pimiento
1 can (10½ ounces)
uncondensed cream of
mushroom soup
(optional)

1¼ cups milk
½ cup rice
½ teaspoon poultry
seasoning
¼ teaspoon salt
1 cup soft bread crumbs
2 tablespoons melted
butter

☐Preheat oven to 300°F.
Brown sausage and drain off excess fat. Add celery, onion, and green pepper. Sauté until tender but not brown. Stir in pimiento, soup (optional), milk, rice, poultry seasoning, and salt. Pour into a casserole and bake, uncovered, for 50 minutes. Mix crumbs and butter; and sprinkle over casserole and bake for 20 minutes longer.

Betty Pursley
Pontiac, Michigan

Dave's Note: Would also make a good stuffing.

ST. PAUL'S RICE

This recipe was given to me by one of my favorite aunts, Peg Stedman of Warwick, Rhode Island, right after I was married fifteen years ago. It's still one of my family's favorites. I have *never* seen it in any other cookbook, and I'm always being asked for the recipe. It can be frozen, too. Do trust you will like it as well as everyone else over the past fifteen years.

1 cup long-grain rice
2 packages chicken noodle soup
2½ cups boiling water
1 pound bulk pork sausage, crumbled
1 large onion, grated

3 to 4 stalks celery, chopped
1 green pepper, chopped
Paprika
Almonds, chopped or slivered (optional)

☐Preheat oven to 350°F.

Add rice and soup to boiling water; boil until mixture is absorbed. Brown sausage; add onion, celery, and pepper. Simmer for a few minutes. Mix together all the ingredients and place in a casserole dish, topped with paprika and almonds. Bake, uncovered, for 1 hour or more.

Julie L. Rain
Bow, New Hampshire

SAUSAGE RAGOÛT

1 pound sweet Italian sausages
1 onion, chopped
1 clove garlic, crushed
1 tablespoon butter

½ pound fresh mushrooms, sliced
1 can (16 ounces) tomatoes
1 small head lettuce, shredded

1 teaspoon salt
Pinch of pepper
2½ cups meat stock or
  bouillon, hot

1 cup alphabet macaroni
1 package (10 ounces)
  frozen peas
2 pimientos, diced

☐Preheat oven to 425°F.

Remove sausage skin and section sausages in small balls; brown lightly in pan. Remove fat and add onion, garlic, butter, and mushrooms. Sauté briefly. Add tomatoes, lettuce, seasonings, and hot stock. Stir, bring to a boil, and add macaroni and pimientos. Stir well and place in a large casserole dish. Cover and bake for 30 minutes. Add more bouillon if necessary for more juice.

Makes 6 to 8 servings.

Carlee L. Howe
Burlington, Massachusetts

SPAGHETTI PIE

5 tablespoons butter
½ cup chopped onion
¼ cup chopped green
  pepper
½ pound ground beef
½ pound Italian sausage,
  casings removed
1 jar (16 ounces) meatless
  spaghetti sauce

6 ounces spaghetti
⅓ cup grated Parmesan
  cheese
2 eggs, well beaten
1 cup cottage cheese
½ cup shredded
  mozzarella cheese

☐Preheat oven to 350°F. Butter a 10-inch pie plate.

Melt 3 tablespoons of the butter in a large skillet over medium-high heat. Add onion and green pepper and sauté until tender, about 5 minutes. Stir in beef and sausages and cook until browned, about 10 minutes. Drain off excess fat. Stir in spaghetti sauce.

Cook spaghetti al dente (about 8 minutes). Rinse and drain. Add remaining butter to pasta and toss until butter is melted. Blend Parmesan cheese and eggs into pasta. Transfer to prepared pie plate and shape into crust. Spread cottage cheese over crust and pour meat mixture over top. Bake until set, about 20 minutes. Sprinkle mozzarella evenly over top and continue baking until cheese melts.

Makes 6 to 8 servings.

Dave's

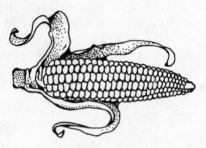

CORN AND SAUSAGE CASSEROLE

2 cans (17 ounces each) cream-style corn	1 cup (13 ounces) evaporated milk
¼ cup chopped green pepper	½ teaspoon salt
¼ cup chopped onion	¼ teaspoon pepper
½ cup cracker crumbs	2 tablespoons butter
	12 sausages

☐Preheat oven to 350°F.

Mix together corn, green pepper, and onion and place half of the mixture in the bottom of a casserole dish. Sprinkle ¼ cup cracker crumbs over this and add remaining vegetable mixture; sprinkle again with ¼ cup cracker crumbs. Mix together evaporated milk, salt, and pepper and pour over casserole; dot with butter. Bake for 30 to 40 minutes.

Cook and brown sausages. Drain off fat and serve on top of casserole.

Makes 6 servings.

Mary MacGillivray
Brighton, Massachusetts

VERMICELLI WITH SALAMI AND CHEESE

8 ounces vermicelli or
  spaghetti
1 can (6 ounces) marinated
  artichoke hearts
2 cloves garlic, minced or
  pressed
⅓ cup vegetable oil
⅓ cup white wine vinegar
1 teaspoon oregano
1 teaspoon dried basil
¼ teaspoon dried
  rosemary

¼ teaspoon black pepper
1½ teaspoons dry mustard
1 medium carrot, pared
  and finely diced
1 small zucchini, pared and
  finely diced
3 ounces sliced salami,
  julienned
2 cups grated mozzarella
  cheese
⅓ plus ¼ cup grated
  Parmesan cheese

☐ Preheat oven to 350°F.

Cook pasta in boiling salted water as package directs. Drain.

Into a large bowl drain marinade from artichokes, reserving hearts. Add garlic, oil, vinegar, oregano, basil, rosemary, pepper, and dry mustard to the bowl. Add pasta and stir. Add finely diced carrot and zucchini, julienned salami, mozzarella, the ⅓ cup Parmesan, and the artichoke hearts. Stir. Spoon mixture into an ungreased shallow 3-quart casserole dish. Cover and bake for about 45 minutes.

Uncover casserole and sprinkle with the ¼ cup Parmesan cheese. Bake 15 minutes longer, or until center is hot.

Makes about 6 servings.

Dave's

Dave's Note: To serve cold, line a bowl with lettuce leaves and spoon mixture into center; garnish with tomato wedges. Chill if made ahead; serve at room temperature.

BEST, WURST SAUERKRAUT

3 thick strips bacon, cut in
   half
½ pound small country
   sausages
1 large onion, chopped
1 medium carrot, pared
   and finely diced
1 tablespoon minced fresh
   parsley
2 pounds sauerkraut
10 juniper berries, crushed
⅔ cup water
½ cup dry German white
   wine

1 large bay leaf, bruised
¾ teaspoon caraway seed
Freshly ground pepper
4 medium potatoes, pared
   and cut into ¼-inch
   slices
Salt to taste
1 pound assorted German
   sausages (bockwurst,
   wienerwurst, blutwurst,
   and knockwurst)
1 tablespoon snipped fresh
   chives

☐ Cook bacon in a large Dutch oven or flameproof casserole over medium-high heat until crisp. Remove and drain on paper towels. Add country sausages to the pan and brown thoroughly on all sides. Remove with slotted spoon and drain. Combine onion, carrot, and parsley in same pan and sauté over medium heat for 4 to 5 minutes. Rinse and drain sauerkraut and add to pan with juniper berries, water, wine, bay leaf, caraway seed, and ¼ teaspoon pepper. Mix well and reduce heat to low. Arrange potatoes on top of pan and season lightly with salt and pepper. Top potatoes with bacon strips and country sausages. Cover and cook gently over low heat for about 20 minutes, watching carefully to prevent sticking.

Just before serving, arrange assorted sausages over top of casserole. Cover and cook until sausages are lightly steamed (do not allow to split), about 10 minutes. Sprinkle with chives and serve immediately.

Makes 5 servings.

Dave's

LOW-CALORIE SPANISH KRAUT

3 slices bacon, chopped
1 onion, chopped
2 pounds sauerkraut,
   rinsed and drained

½ cup (packed) brown
   sugar
1 can (16 ounces) tomatoes

☐Preheat oven to 350°F.

Brown bacon, then onion. Drain off grease. Add sauerkraut, tomatoes and sugar. Cook, uncovered, until slightly thickened. Pour into a greased casserole dish. Bake for 30 minutes. Makes 8 servings.

Mrs. C. Kintner
Saginaw, Michigan

OLD FAITHFUL

This is great fixed the night before, half cooked, then finished after getting home . . . quick, easy, and delicious.

1½ pounds boneless pork
   loin or lamb, cut in
   cubes
1 cup rice
1 can (16 ounces) whole
   tomatoes (or 6 fresh, in
   season)
1 green pepper, seeded and
   thinly sliced

1 onion, sliced in thin rings
Sage to taste
Thyme to taste
Garlic powder to taste
Salt and pepper to taste
1 can (10½ ounces) beef
   consommé
¼ soup can burgundy
   (optional)

☐Preheat oven to 350°F.

Mix rice, tomatoes, green pepper, onion, and half of spices and place in a 1½-quart casserole dish. Put meat on top of rice mixture and sprinkle remaining spices on top. Pour consommé over

all. (You may want to add wine.) Cover and bake for 1 hour.
Uncover and cook for 30 minutes longer. (Check to make sure
rice is cooked.)

Makes 6 to 8 servings.

Marie Foss
Rockport, Massachusetts

GRANDMA'S OLD-FASHIONED CHICKEN AND STUFFING
(Czechoslovakian)

4 to 5 cups cubed day-old Italian bread	1 teaspoon salt
1 cup milk	½ bunch fresh parsley, chopped
1 teaspoon poultry seasoning	2 eggs
½ teaspoon ground black pepper	1 chicken, cut up
	4 tablespoons butter, melted

☐ To make stuffing, place cubed Italian bread in a medium bowl
and soak in milk for 1 hour. Add poultry seasoning, pepper, salt,
parsley, and eggs and mix well.

Preheat oven to 375°F.

Place chicken pieces in a shallow baking dish and spread
stuffing on top of chicken. Bake, uncovered, for 30 minutes, until
stuffing is golden brown. Baste with melted butter from time to
time to bring out the golden brown color.

Makes 4 to 6 servings.

Louise Morin
Bradford, Massachusetts

CHICKEN DELICIOUS CASSEROLE

This is my favorite chicken casserole. It is always very popular at our church suppers. The water chestnuts give it a nice texture and the cornbread stuffing topping gives it a really yummy flavor.

1½ cups finely diced celery
1 can (10½ ounces) cream
   of mushroom soup
1 cup mayonnaise
2 cans (5 ounces each)
   water chestnuts, drained
   and sliced

4 whole chicken breasts,
   boned, cooked, and
   thinly sliced
1 package cornbread
   stuffing
¾ cup butter, melted

☐Preheat oven to 350°F.

Cook celery in boiling water until tender. Drain, then mix with the soup, mayonnaise, and water chestnuts in a bowl. Lightly grease a 13×9-inch pan and place sliced chicken on bottom. Pour soup mixture on top. Mix stuffing with melted butter and sprinkle on top. Bake for 30 minutes, or until bubbly and brown on top.

Makes 8 servings.

Virginia D. Ricker
Haverhill, Massachusetts

CHICKEN CASSEROLE

1 cup rice
1 can (10½ ounces) cream
   of chicken soup
1 can (10½ ounces) cream
   of mushroom soup
½ envelope onion soup
   mix

1 soup can of water
1 chicken (2½ to 3
   pounds), cut up
Salt and pepper to taste
   (optional)

☐Preheat oven to 375°F.

Place rice in a 2½- or 3-quart casserole. Combine canned soup, soup mix, and water in bowl and mix well. Pour over rice. Place chicken on top and season if desired. Cover and bake for 2 hours. Remove cover and bake for 30 minutes longer.

Makes 4 to 6 servings.

Mrs. Claire Cabana
Taunton, Massachusetts

CHICKEN SANS SOUCI

1 tablespoon vegetable oil
1 tablespoon butter
2 frying chickens, cut up
3 tablespoons flour
1 can (10½ ounces) consommé
1 cup Sauternes

¾ to 1 cup canned mushrooms with juice
3 tablespoons chopped onion
3 tablespoons parsley
1 teaspoon Accent (optional)

☐Preheat oven to 350°F.

Heat oil and butter in heavy skillet. Brown chicken on both sides, then remove to casserole. Add flour to drippings. Add consommé and wine and cook stirring, until thick. Add remaining ingredients. Pour sauce over chicken, cover, and bake about 2 hours. Turn and baste at least twice during baking.

Makes 8 servings.

Dave's

Dave's Note: This is an easy, prepare in advance, never fail recipe. I should call it Chicken Aunt Kat, but she probably wouldn't hear of it. I also bake it covered with aluminum foil and don't turn it at all!

GLORIOUS CHICKEN

This recipe was given to me by a friend in Los Altos, California, who had tasted it at a dinner party and asked her hostess for the recipe. It's easy to make and tastes gourmet and expensive.

2 packages (10 ounces each) frozen French-cut green beans, thawed
4 whole large chicken breasts, cooked, boned, and slivered
1 can (10½ ounces) cream of celery soup

1 can (10½ ounces) cream of chicken soup
2 cups sour cream
½ envelope onion soup mix
1 package chicken-flavored Rice-a-Roni

☐Preheat oven to 350°F.
Spread beans in a 13×9-inch casserole dish. Top with chicken meat. Combine soups, sour cream, and onion soup mix. Pour over chicken. Prepare Rice-a-Roni as directed on package and layer over casserole. Bake for 1 hour 15 minutes.
Makes 8 servings.

Mrs. Saul Scheff
Brookline, Massachusetts

CHICKEN CASSEROLE

½ cup diced cooked chicken or turkey
½ cup cashews or almonds
1 cup chopped celery
1 can (8 ounces) Chinese noodles

¼ cup minced onion
¼ cup chicken broth
1 can (10½ ounces) cream of mushroom soup
Peas and mushrooms to taste

☐Preheat oven to 325°F.

Toss all ingredients lightly in a casserole dish, saving half of the noodles for top. Bake for 30 minutes.

Makes 4 servings.

Lucille Townsend
Columbus, Indiana

CHICKEN HAZELLE

1 cup all-purpose flour
½ teaspoon salt
¼ teaspoon freshly
    ground pepper
1 frying chicken (2½ to 3½
    pounds), cut into 6
    pieces
¼ cup olive oil
4 large tomatoes, peeled,
    seeded, and chopped

4 ounces lean ham, diced
1 jar (4 ounces) pimientos
    or 1 small roasted
    pepper, peeled, seeded,
    and chopped
½ cup dry white wine
Chopped fresh parsley
Freshly cooked rice
    (enough for 4 to 6
    people)

☐If planning to bake chicken, preheat oven to 350°F.

Combine flour, salt, and pepper in a medium bowl. Dredge chicken pieces in flour mixture, shaking off excess. Heat oil in a large skillet over medium heat. Add chicken and brown on all sides. Transfer to a 3- or 4-quart baking dish with a tight-fitting lid (or set aside for stovetop cooking).

Drain oil from skillet. Add tomatoes and ham and cook over medium heat, stirring frequently, for 5 minutes. Stir in pimientos. Add wine and simmer, uncovered, for 3 to 4 minutes. Pour over chicken in dish (or return chicken to skillet). Cover and bake (or cook over low heat) until chicken is cooked through, about 25 minutes. Garnish with chopped parsley and serve immediately over rice.

Makes 4 to 6 servings.

Dave's

ORANGE CHICKEN AND RICE

1 cup rice	½ cup cream of
6 chicken parts	mushroom soup
1 cup orange juice	½ envelope onion soup
¼ cup sherry	mix

☐Preheat oven to 350°F.

Butter a casserole dish and place rice in bottom. Cover with chicken parts. Mix orange juice, sherry, and mushroom soup and pour over chicken. Sprinkle with onion soup mix. Cover with foil and bake for 2 hours. Remove foil and bake for another 15 minutes. If rice seems too dry, add a little water.

Makes 3 servings.

Eva Baltteim
Cranston, Rhode Island

CHICKEN EN CASSEROLE

This is a lovely company meal. It can be prepared ahead of time and frozen or can be made and served immediately. Leftovers, if there are any, reheat well.

10 ounces sharp cheddar cheese	½ cup chopped onion
4 whole chicken breasts, boned and skinned	2 tablespoons all-purpose flour
2 eggs, beaten	1 teaspoon salt
¾ cup fine dry bread crumbs	¼ teaspoon pepper
⅓ cup butter	1 cup chicken bouillon
½ cup chopped green pepper	3 cups cooked rice (wild and white mixed)
	1 can (3 ounces) sliced mushrooms, drained

☐Preheat oven to 400°F.

Cut cheese into 8 equal stick portions. Cut chicken breasts in half and flatten to ¼-inch thickness. Roll each half breast around a stick of cheese. Dip in egg and then bread crumbs. Brown chicken in butter; remove and set aside.

Sauté green pepper and onion in butter until tender; add flour, seasonings, and bouillon. Cook, uncovered, stirring, until thickened. Add rice and mushrooms. Pour into a shallow, 8×8×2-inch casserole dish. Top with chicken and bake for 20 minutes.

Makes 8 servings.

Alice Blauss
West Hanover, Massachusetts

SKILLET-ROASTED TURKEY

1 tablespoon salad oil
1 tablespoon butter
4 pounds turkey thighs, drumsticks and hindquarters
2 large onions, chopped
2 large cloves garlic, minced or pressed
1 cup dry red wine or chicken broth
1 can (10½ ounces) condensed mushroom soup

1 teaspoon each dried basil, thyme leaves, and rubbed sage
1 tablespoon Dijon mustard
6 to 8 each small whole carrots, small thin-skinned potatoes, and small boiling onions
3 tablespoons each cornstarch and water
Salt and pepper to taste

☐Preheat oven to 325°F.

In a large frying pan, heat oil and butter over medium high heat. Add turkey pieces and cook until browned on all sides; remove pieces as they are browned and arrange them in a 6- to 8-quart casserole or Dutch oven.

To fat in frying pan add onions and garlic; cook until onion is limp. Then add wine, soup, basil, thyme, sage, and mustard. Bring to a boil, stirring often, then pour over the turkey. Cover and bake for 1 hour.

Add to the pan carrots, potatoes, and onions, making sure they are coated with liquid. Return to the oven for about 1 hour, or until meat and vegetables are tender. Lift the vegetables and meat out onto a serving plate. Cover and keep warm. Skim fat from cooking liquid, then add a mixture of the cornstarch and water, blended until smooth, Cook, stirring, until it boils and thickens. Season to taste with salt and pepper. Serve some sauce on meat. Put more in gravy boat.

Makes 8 servings.

Dave's

TURKEY AND WHITE BEANS

1 pound dried white beans
6 slices bacon, diced
4 pounds turkey thighs,
    drumsticks, or
    hindquarters
½ cup dry white wine or
    chicken broth
2 large onions, chopped
3 cloves garlic, minced or
    pressed
4 medium carrots, pared
    and sliced ¼ inch thick

2 stalks celery, sliced ¼
    inch thick
1 can (14½ ounces) plum
    tomatoes or equivalent
    in sliced fresh baby
    tomatoes
1½ teaspoons rosemary
    leaves
Salt and pepper to taste

☐Preheat oven to 350°F.

Soak and cook the dried beans as directed on the package. Drain and set aside (you should have 5 to 6 cups).

In a large frying pan, cook the bacon until crisp. Remove bacon, drain, and set aside. Add the turkey pieces to the pan drippings; cook over medium-high heat, turning until browned all over. Transfer turkey pieces as they are browned to a 6-quart casserole dish or Dutch oven. Pour wine or broth over turkey, cover, and bake for about 1 hour.

Meanwhile, add the onions and garlic to frying pan; cook, stirring, until the onion is limp. Add carrots, celery, tomatoes, rosemary, and cooked beans. Bring to a boil, then season to taste with salt and pepper.

After turkey has baked for 1 hour, remove it from oven and pour hot bean mixture on top. Cover and continue baking for 45 to 60 minutes, or until turkey is tender. Let stand for about 15 minutes before serving. Garnish with the bacon.

Makes about 8 servings.

Dave's

Dave's Note: Don't use white meat of turkey. Dark meat is cheaper and better tasting.

TURKEY DIVAN

3 tablespoons unsalted butter	¾ cup grated Parmesan cheese
1 small onion, finely chopped	¼ cup grated Swiss cheese
¼ cup all-purpose flour	¾ pound turkey breast, thinly sliced
2 cups milk, hot	Salt and freshly ground pepper to taste
1 bunch broccoli	
2 egg yolks, at room temperature	

☐Preheat oven to 375°F.

Melt butter in a large, heavy saucepan over medium heat. When foam subsides, add onion and sauté until transparent, about 5 minutes. Add flour; cook, stirring constantly, for 3 minutes (do not let flour burn). Gradually whisk in ½ cup of the hot milk until mixture is smooth. Whisk in remaining milk and bring to a boil. Reduce heat and simmer, uncovered, stirring frequently, until sauce is smooth and thickened, about 10 minutes.

Meanwhile, wash, trim, and pare stems of broccoli and cut into ½-inch cubes. Cook broccoli in a large saucepan of salted boiling water (or steam over the water) until crisp-tender, about 8 minutes. Drain, then rinse under cold running water. Drain again thoroughly.

Strain sauce through fine-mesh sieve into bowl. While still hot, whisk in egg yolks, one at a time. Stir in ½ cup of the grated Parmesan and all the Swiss cheese, one third at a time, stirring after each addition until smooth. Season with salt and pepper. Divide broccoli among four individual baking dishes and top with overlapping slices of turkey. Spoon sauce over turkey. Top with remaining Parmesan cheese, dividing evenly. Bake until sauce is golden brown and slightly bubbly around the edges, about 15 minutes.

Makes 4 servings.

Dave's

CHICKEN AND SHRIMP CURRY CASSEROLE

1 package (7 ounces) noodles Romanoff mix
1 can (10½ ounces) cream of celery soup
1 cup milk
2 tablespoons butter or margarine

1 teaspoon curry powder
1 cup cooked, cubed chicken
½ pound cooked shrimp
1 can (3 ounces) mushroom slices

☐Preheat oven to 350°F. Cook noodles according to package directions. Drain well and transfer to 1½-quart baking dish. Combine sauce mix, soup, and milk in a medium saucepan and bring to a boil over medium-high heat. Stir in butter and curry powder. Reduce heat and simmer, uncovered, for 10 minutes.

Add chicken, shrimp, and mushrooms. Pour mixture over noodles and blend well. Cover and bake until heated through, about 30 minutes. Serve immediately.

4 servings.

Dave's

SEAFOOD CASSEROLE

1 small onion, chopped
1 tablespoon chopped
  green pepper
1 teaspoon margarine
2 ounces sliced pimiento,
  drained
⅔ cup milk
1 can (10½ ounces) New
  England clam chowder

1 can (10½ ounces) cream
  of celery soup
1 teaspoon lemon juice
1 can (7 ounces) tuna,
  drained
1 can (7 ounces) pink
  salmon, drained
Frozen Tater Tots

☐ Preheat oven to 350°F.

Sauté onion and green pepper in margarine for 2 to 3 minutes. Add all of the remaining ingredients, except tater tots, and heat through. In the bottom of a large casserole, layer tater tots one deep. Pour warm seafood mixture over top and top with another layer of tater tots. Bake for 30 minutes.

Mrs. Jeanette Wicherts
Sterling, Illinois

BAKED CATFISH SUPREME

4 thick catfish fillets
5 tablespoons lemon juice
1 teaspoon salt
½ teaspoon white pepper

1½ cups mayonnaise
¼ cup sweet relish
2 medium onions, finely
  chopped

1 teaspoon chopped fresh
parsley
1 teaspoon chopped celery
leaves
Dash of paprika

¼ cup fine dry bread
crumbs
2 tablespoons grated
cheddar cheese

☐Marinate fish in lemon juice for 25 minutes.
Preheat oven to 350°F.
Drain fish and place in lightly greased casserole dish. Mix salt,
pepper, mayonnaise, relish, onions, parsley, and celery leaves
and spread over fish, coating well. Mix paprika, crumbs, and
cheese and sprinkle over top. Bake for 25 to 30 minutes.
Makes 4 servings.

Margaret Strescino
Gloucester, Massachusetts

HADDOCK CHÂTEAU

1 whole haddock (5 pounds)
4 cups milk
9 tablespoons butter or
margarine
7 tablespoons all-purpose
flour

½ pound Borden's
Chateau cheese, grated
¼ cup sherry
Bread crumbs

☐Boil or steam whole fish for 30 minutes. Preheat oven to
350 °F. Remove head of fish, pick out bones and skin. Keep
fish in large pieces and place in a 1½-to-2-quart casserole.
Make white sauce by melting 7 tablespoons of the butter over
low heat; gradually stir in flour until smooth; add milk, stirring
constantly; cook until thick. Add grated cheese and sherry and
pour sauce over fish. Cover with crumbs and dot with remaining
2 tablespoons of butter, cut in pieces. Bake for 30 minutes.
Makes 6 to 8 servings.

Mrs. Karl O. Trask
Holden, Massachusetts

QUICK SEAFOOD CASSEROLE

1 pound flounder fillets
1 package (12 ounces)
   langostinos, thawed
6 tablespoons sherry wine
1 can Newburg sauce
½ stick margarine,
   melted

2 cups soft fresh bread
   crumbs
1 teaspoon dehydrated
   onion
2 tablespoons grated
   Parmesan cheese

☐Preheat oven to 400°F.

Halve flounder fillets lengthwise. Wrap fish around langostinos and place close together in flat casserole dish. Sprinkle 4 tablespoons of the sherry over all, then pour on Newburg sauce. Melt margarine in saucepan over low heat and add crumbs, onion, cheese, and remaining 2 tablespoons sherry. Pour on top of casserole and bake for 30 minutes.

Makes 4 servings.

Mary Pagliarini
Peabody, Massachusetts

NETTA'S HADDOCK CASSEROLE

My haddock casserole was given to me by my hairdresser, Netta Frank. When I go there, I always bring a paper and pen. She is a super cook and I have many a great recipe from her. I have had this recipe for about two years, and every time I make it, I have to give it to someone else. Everyone loves it.

2 pounds haddock fillets
Dijon mustard (enough to
  coat fish)
Dillweed to taste
1 can (10½ ounces) cream
  of celery soup

½ pound cheddar
  cheese, grated
Chopped fresh parsley
Paprika to taste

☐ Preheat oven to 400°F.

Smear Dijon mustard on both sides of fish. Sprinkle with dillweed and place in a casserole dish. Add cream of celery soup and
top with grated cheddar cheese. Sprinkle with chopped parsley
and paprika to cover. Bake for 20 minutes.

Makes 4 to 6 servings.

Ellie Lashua
Kennebunk, Maine

LABRADOR CASSEROLE OF HADDOCK

This casserole comes to me from a visiting nurse (also named
Hope) who made her rounds by horse and buggy in rural New
Hampshire in the early 1900s. She knew all about gourmet cooking, but it was called "economy" or "thrifty" in those days. This
was a frequent meal in my childhood days, and the recipe has
been passed on to my daughters and granddaughters.

1½ pounds fillet of
  haddock
1 clove garlic, halved
Salt and pepper to taste
3 tablespoons lemon juice
½ cup vegetable oil

1½ cups sliced onion
2 cups drained canned
  tomatoes
1½ tablespoons minced
  fresh parsley

☐ Preheat oven to 375°F.

Rub fish with cut garlic and sprinkle with salt and pepper. Place
in a buttered casserole dish. Combine lemon juice and oil and

pour over fish. Top with sliced onion, tomatoes, and parsley. Cover and bake for 30 minutes. Remove cover and bake 15 minutes longer, basting twice with liquor in casserole. Serve with rice.

Makes 4 servings.

Hope C. Ayers
Wenham, Massachusetts

SALMON CASSEROLE

Been in the family for over seventy years.

1 can (15½ ounces) red
   salmon
10 saltines

Milk or sour cream to
   cover

☐Preheat oven to 350°F.

Clean salmon and place in small buttered casserole. Break up with fork. Crush saltines and add, stirring gently to mix. Cover with milk or sour cream. Cook for 25 minutes.

Makes 2 servings.

Ms. Ruth J. Alexander
Worcester, Massachusetts

Dave's Note: Too much preparation!

SALMON SCALLOP

Do not parboil potatoes before placing in casserole dish, as it will detract from the flavor. This recipe has been in my family for quite a while. I'm pushing eighty.

4 large potatoes
1 or 2 cans (15½ ounces
   each) salmon

2 onions, sliced thinly
2 tablespoons butter or
   margarine

2 tablespoons flour
½ cup milk
½ cup light cream

½ teaspoon salt
½ teaspoon white pepper
2 teaspoons lemon juice

☐Preheat oven to 350°F.

Pare potatoes. Slice and lay half in the bottom of a 2-quart casserole. Layer the salmon on top of the potatoes and then the onions. Top with remaining potatoes. Melt butter in a saucepan over low heat and slowly blend in flour. Add milk gradually, stirring constantly until thickened. Add salt, pepper, and lemon juice and pour sauce over potatoes. Bake until potatoes are tender, about 1 hour.

Mrs. Evelyn Collins
Jamaica Plain, Massachusetts

RICE AND TUNA CASSEROLE

2 cups cooked rice
1 can (7 ounces) tuna (white meat)
1 medium onion, sliced
Chopped celery (optional)

1 can (10½ ounces) asparagus soup (or cream of mushroom soup)
Milk (optional)

☐Preheat oven to 350°F.

Place layer of rice in bottom of casserole, then a layer of half the tuna, sliced onion, and celery; repeat. Pour soup over all and lightly mix. Bake for about 30 minutes. Add a little milk if it appears to dry out.

Makes 4 servings.

Mrs. John Murphy
Athol, Massachusetts

TUNA CASSEROLE
(Casserole Poulet de la Mer)

This recipe makes a good Sunday night supper.

4 ounces cooked egg
  noodles
1 can (10½ ounces) cream
  of mushroom soup
½ cup sour cream
1 package (10 ounces)
  frozen peas and carrots,
  cooked and drained
½ cup sliced fresh
  mushrooms

1 can (13 ounces) tuna,
  drained
1 teaspoon dried thyme
½ teaspoon salt
¼ teaspoon pepper
¾ cup seasoned fine dry
  bread crumbs
3 tablespoons butter or
  margarine, melted

☐ Preheat oven to 350°F.
   Combine cooked noodles, soup, and sour cream in a large
bowl. Add cooked peas and carrots, mushrooms, tuna, thyme,
salt, and pepper. Pour into an oiled 1½-quart casserole dish.
Combine bread crumbs and melted butter and sprinkle over top.
Bake, uncovered, for 25 to 30 minutes, or until hot and bubbly.
   Makes 4 servings.

Jeanette Proulx
North Reading, Massachusetts

RICE CURRY AND FLOUNDER CASSEROLE

I cook creatively a great deal, and the flavor of curry certainly
complements this casserole. Delighted to share this recipe with
all you great cooks.

1 cup long-grain rice
Scant 2 cups water
4 flounder fillets, rolled
⅛ teaspoon salt

1 teaspoon curry powder
1 cup curry-flavored
  whipped cream
Cooked shrimp

☐Preheat oven to 350°F.

Place all of the ingredients, except whipped cream and shrimp, in a large buttered casserole dish. Cover and bake for 30 minutes. Remove from oven and spread whipped cream (with a little curry powder folded in) on top. Garnish with peeled shrimp. Serve at once.

Makes 4 servings.

Raye T. Patrone
Johnston, Rhode Island

FISH CASSEROLE

1 medium onion, sliced
1 clove garlic, minced
2 fresh medium tomatoes, sliced
1 cup chopped fresh parsley
½ cup margarine

2 pounds white fish fillets
½ teaspoon salt
¼ teaspoon pepper
½ teaspoon dried oregano
½ cup bread crumbs

☐Preheat oven to 350°F.

In a large skillet, sauté onion, garlic, tomatoes, and parsley in ¼ cup of the margarine; set aside. Arrange fish in a large greased baking dish and sprinkle with salt, pepper, and oregano. Arrange sautéed mixture over fish. Sprinkle crumbs evenly over all. Dot with remaining margarine. Bake, covered, for 35 to 40 minutes, or until fish is fork-tender.

Makes 6 to 8 servings.

Mrs. Robert Shipley
Dennisport, Massachusetts

NORWEGIAN FISH PUDDING

This recipe was handed down by my mother and grandmother, who came from Norway. While my children were growing up they even asked for it for their birthday dinner. Even people who don't particularly like fish seem to like this dish; I've even used pollock in it. The casserole bakes in the time it takes to bake potatoes, which are the perfect complement.

1½ pounds haddock or cod
    fillets
1 egg
1 tablespoon all-purpose
    flour

1 cup milk
Salt and pepper to taste
Pinch of sugar
Butter or margarine

☐Preheat oven to 350°F.
  Boil fish in salted water until flaky. Drain and mash with potato masher. Add remaining ingredients, except butter. Place in a greased casserole and dot generously with butter (mixture will be slushy.) Bake in a 350°F oven for 1 hour, until golden brown. Serve with melted butter and chives on the side.
  Makes 6 servings.

Mrs. William W. Trout
Kingston, Massachusetts

CRABMEAT IMPERIAL

1 green pepper, finely
    diced
2 pimientos, finely diced
1 tablespoon prepared
    English mustard
1 teaspoon salt

½ teaspoon white pepper
2 eggs
1 cup mayonnaise
3 pounds lump crabmeat
Paprika

☐Preheat oven to 350°F.
  Mix green pepper and pimientos and add all the other ingredi-

ents except paprika, mixing with fingers so crab lumps aren't broken. Divide mixture into 8 crabshells or casseroles, heaping it in lightly. Top with a little coating of mayonnaise and sprinkle with paprika. Bake for 15 minutes. Serve hot or cold. Makes 8 servings.

Mrs. Lida Campbell
Elsie, Michigan

CRAB CASSEROLE

4 tablespoons butter
2 tablespoons all-purpose
  flour
1 pound crabmeat
2 teaspoons lemon juice
½ teaspoon prepared
  horseradish
1 cup whole milk

1 teaspoon chopped fresh
  parsley
1 teaspoon prepared
  mustard
1 cup grated sharp cheese
1 teaspoon salt
½ cup buttered bread
  crumbs

☐Preheat oven to 400°F.

Melt butter in a large saucepan and add flour, stirring until smooth. Add all the other ingredients except buttered bread crumbs. Mix well; pour into a greased casserole and sprinkle with the buttered crumbs. Bake for 20 minutes; it may stand longer and not spoil.

Makes 4 servings.

Mrs. John F. Vey
Fremont, New Hampshire

VICKI'S DEVILED CRAB CASSEROLE

This crab casserole is especially delicious, and has been my most popular "creation" with all my family and friends. I would think that considering the part of the country you live in and the availability of lobster, the same dish would be equally delicious with bits of lobster.

1 cup finely chopped celery
1 green pepper, seeded and finely chopped
1 cup finely chopped green onion
½ cup finely chopped fresh parsley
1 teaspoon salt

1½ tablespoons dry mustard
Dash of Tabasco
2 pounds backfin crabmeat
1½ cups crushed soda crackers
½ cup cream
1½ cups butter, melted

☐Preheat oven to 350°F.

In a large bowl, combine all ingredients except crackers, cream, and butter. Toss lightly with crushed crackers. Place in a buttered casserole dish. Pour cream and ½ cup melted butter over the mixture and toss with more cracker crumbs. Pour remaining butter over all. Bake for about 30 minutes, until browned.

Makes 6 to 8 servings.

Vicki E. Sharp
Johnstown, Pennsylvania

Dave's Note: Lobster is available—so is gold bullion.

LOBSTER CASSEROLE

1 pound fresh mushrooms, sliced
3 tablespoons all-purpose flour

1 teaspoon salt
⅛ teaspoon paprika
1½ cups milk
½ cup chicken bouillon

2 cups lobster meat
½ cup cream
2 egg yolks, beaten well

½ cup buttered bread
crumbs

☐Preheat oven to 450°F.
Slice mushrooms and sauté in butter for 2 minutes. Add flour, salt, and paprika. Blend thoroughly and cook, stirring, for 5 minutes. Stir in bouillon and milk and cook for 3 minutes, stirring constantly. Add lobster meat, cream, and well-beaten egg yolks. Cook over low heat, stirring well, for 3 minutes. Pour into a buttered casserole dish and cover with buttered crumbs. Bake for 10 minutes.
Makes 4 to 6 servings.

M. V. Carson
Quincy, Massachusetts

SEAFOOD POTPOURRI

Walk along a beautiful ocean beach and collect large sea clam shells for your "dishes." Recycle them for nut dishes, ashtrays, soap holders, etc.

4 shallots, finely diced
8 tablespoons butter
¼ teaspoon dried thyme
¼ teaspoon nutmeg
Salt and pepper to taste
Pinch of cayenne
¼ cup all-purpose flour
2 cans (7½ ounces each)
    clams or 1 cup fresh
    clams plus broth (can
    substitute lobster, crab,
    langostinos)

¼ cup dry white wine
    mixed with the juices of
    the clams, plus enough
    cream to measure 2
    cups
¼ cup coarsely chopped
    water chestnuts
½ cup cooked rice
¾ cup peas
¼ pound fresh
    mushrooms, coarsely
    chopped

⅓ cup grated Swiss
  cheese
⅓ cup fresh bread
  crumbs

6 to 8 lightly buttered
  cooked large pasta
  shells

☐Preheat oven to 425°F.

Sauté the shallots in 4 tablespoons of the butter. Blend in the thyme, nutmeg, salt, pepper, cayenne, and the flour. Cook for 2 minutes. Add the clam juices or stock and the white wine and cream, stir until thickened. Remove from heat. Add clams, water chestnuts, peas, and rice.

Sauté mushrooms in 2 tablespoons of butter and add to the clam mixture. Put the clam mixture in the buttered shells. Top with a mixture of the Swiss cheese and bread crumbs. Dot with remaining 2 tablespoons butter. (It can be frozen at this point and taken out as needed.) Bake for 15 to 20 minutes, until nicely browned.

Makes 6 to 8 servings.

Priscilla Nelson
Wakefield, Rhode Island

CLAMS À LA CASTILLIAN
(Clams à la Bay of Biscay)

I was born in the province of Santander (near the Bay of Biscay in northern Spain.) My aunt, Sinforosa Higuera Gomez Casar, was chosen from twenty-five peasant women from northern Spain to be the "wet" nurse to La Infanta Maria Teresa (daughter of Queen Maria Cristina and King Alfonso XII of Spain.) It was quite an honor in those days. She was a beautiful blonde with blue eyes—not uncommon in northern Spain. When she left the Palace in Madrid, she went to live in Santander. I was a very young girl when she invited our family to visit her. To this day, I remember the delicious meals she served. Especially this recipe for clams and rice. It has been a favorite with my children for many years. It's terrific and simple to make.

2 pounds fresh steamer
   clams
1 clove garlic
2 tablespoons olive oil
2 tablespoons chopped
   fresh flat-leaf (Italian)
   parsley

1 cup long-grain rice
2 cups water
Flat-leaf (Italian) parsley
   sprigs

☐Carefully wash clams—remove the dark vein, etc.—and make sure they are completely free from sand.

In saucepan, sauté garlic clove in hot olive oil. When the garlic is golden brown, remove from oil and discard. Add the clams to the hot olive oil and cook for 10 minutes, stirring gently with wooden spoon. Add chopped parsley and stir again, lowering heat. Add rice to the clams and stir again carefully with wooden spoon. Add water to cover clams and bring to a boil. Lower heat and simmer, covered, for about 25 minutes. Water will disappear and rice will penetrate the now opened clams.

Serve on a large platter. Garnish with parsley. You can just pick up the clam shell and eat right from it.

Makes 4 servings.

Leonor Acebo
Quincy, Massachusetts

MARGUERITE'S CLAM CASSEROLE

As delicious as it is easy, this is almost a soufflé.

4 tablespoons butter
2 cans (7½ ounces each)
   minced clams,
   undrained
1 teaspoon dillweed

2 cups crushed saltines
2 eggs
2 cups milk
Pepper to taste
Paprika to taste

☐Melt butter in a flameproof casserole dish and swirl it around to coat well. In a mixing bowl, combine clams with juice, dillweed, saltines, and eggs, which have been beaten and combined with milk and pepper to taste. Mix together and place in the casserole dish. Sprinkle well with paprika and let the casserole stand for 2 hours.

Preheat oven to 350°F.

Bake casserole for about 30 minutes, or until well set.

Makes 4 servings.

Priscilla Monk
Pembroke, Massachusetts

GRETCHEN AND CRAIG CAMPBELL'S SCALLOPS AND SHRIMP IN CASSEROLE

It's amazing what you can learn from your children! This recipe comes to me from my daughter, Mrs. Craig Campbell of Dallas, Texas. She and her husband are both attorneys and like to entertain elegantly, but simply. She claims that all their guests think they have slaved over a hot stove for hours with this casserole.

½ pound shrimp, peeled
and deveined
½ pound scallops
8 tablespoons butter — *less*
↓ 3 ounces dry white wine
½ pound fresh
mushrooms, sliced
1 green onion, sliced
3 tablespoons all-purpose
flour

3 ounces dry sherry
½ cup milk
1 cup heavy cream *or Light or half half*
1 egg yolk, beaten
Salt and pepper to taste
4 packaged or homemade
pastry shells

☐ Preheat oven to 350°F.

Saute scallops and shrimp in 3 tablespoons of the butter until golden brown. Add white wine, stirring well. Transfer mixture to a buttered casserole. Sauté mushrooms and green onion in 2 tablespoons butter until soft but not browned. Add to casserole.

Melt remaining 3 tablespoons butter in a separate pan. Add flour, blending well. Add sherry and cook gently for a few minutes. Slowly add milk and cream, stirring constantly until well blended. Season to taste with salt and pepper. When sauce has thickened, remove from heat and stir in beaten egg yolk. Pour sauce over scallops, shrimp, mushrooms, and green onion in casserole. Bake for 20 minutes, or until top is browned. Serve in pastry shells. Makes 4 servings.

Ingeborg A. Muench
Marblehead, Massachusetts

EGGS AND MUSHROOMS EN CASSEROLE

½ pound fresh
   mushrooms
1½ cups boiling water
1 tablespoon vegetable
   shortening
4 tablespoons all-purpose
   flour

1 teaspoon salt
Dash of pepper
Dash of cayenne
1 cup milk
6 hard-boiled eggs, sliced
2 tablespoons fine dry
   bread crumbs

☐Preheat oven to 350°F.

Wash mushrooms and remove stems. Cook stems in boiling water for 15 minutes. Strain liquid into cup. Slice mushrooms and sauté slowly in shortening until tender. Mix flour, salt, pepper, and cayenne together in a saucepan and add milk slowly to make a smooth paste. Add the mushroom stock and cook over a low burner, stirring constantly until thick. Add mushrooms. Put a layer of sliced eggs in a casserole dish, then a layer of the mushroom mixture. Repeat until all the ingredients are used. Sprinkle top with bread crumbs. Bake for 20 minutes, or until crumbs are brown.

Makes 4 to 6 servings.

Nelma Carey
East Dennis, Massachusetts

TOFU AND BROWN RICE CASSEROLE

Excellent main dish—economical and healthful.

4½ teaspoons vegetable oil	Dash of pepper
1¼ tablespoons butter	1 cup milk
1½ onions, thinly sliced	½ cup wheat germ
1 cup cooked brown rice	3 ounces cheese of your
12 to 16 ounces tofu	choice, grated

☐Preheat oven to 350°F.

Heat a large skillet and coat with 2 teaspoons of the oil and all the butter. Add onion and sauté until lightly browned. Add brown rice, then tofu (press liquid out), sautéing each for two minutes. Season with pepper. Place tofu-onion mixture in a 1½- to 2-quart casserole coated with remaining 2½ teaspoons oil. Pour in milk; sprinkle with wheat germ and the cheese. Bake for 20 minutes, or until cheese is browned.

Makes 4 servings.

Barbara Champeon
Cape Elizabeth, Maine

GARBANZO CASSEROLE

1 tablespoon vegetable oil	2 tablespoons slivered
1 tablespoon butter or	green pepper
margarine	¼ teaspoon salt
1 medium onion, chopped	1 teaspoon sugar
1 clove garlic, crushed	1 can (20 ounces)
½ cup long-grain rice	garbanzos (chick-peas),
1 cup tomato liquid	drained
4 canned plum tomatoes,	
halved	

☐In a heavy 1½-quart Dutch oven with cover, sauté onion and garlic until golden in the butter and oil, stirring constantly. Add

rice and sauté for a few minutes before adding tomato liquid, balance of vegetables (except chick-peas), salt, and sugar. Cover and cook slowly for 20 minutes, until rice is done. Toss once or twice during this period. Add peas and toss; uncover and allow to sit for 10 minutes to the right consistency.
Makes 4 servings.

Enid Cantoreggi
Norfolk, Massachusetts

NOODLE CASSEROLE

During World War II, when families were limited to a certain number of red meat tokens a month, it was necessary to find sources of protein besides meat. Eggs and cheese became good substitutes. Our family was living in Grand Rapids, Michigan at that time. When round steak went up to, imagine, 45 cents a pound, this recipe provided a welcome money saver, as well as a delicious dinner. A friend in her eighties gave the recipe to me, and I have been using it for over forty years.

½ pound fresh
    mushrooms, sliced
1 green pepper, seeded,
    finely chopped
4 tablespoons butter
2 tablespoons all-purpose
    flour
3 cups milk
Salt and pepper to taste
1 package (7 or 8 ounces)
    wide noodles, cooked

6 hard-boiled eggs, thinly
    sliced
1 bottle (2½ ounces)
    stuffed olives, drained
    and sliced
1 jar (7½ ounces)
    pimientos, drained and
    sliced
½ pound sharp cheddar
    cheese, grated

☐ Sauté mushrooms and green pepper in 2 tablespoons of the butter. Melt remaining 2 tablespoons butter in separate saucepan over low heat; add flour gradually, stirring constantly, and mix until smooth. Slowly pour in milk and season with salt and pepper. Cook until smooth and thick. Add all of the ingredients to the white sauce and serve.

Mrs. Milton M. McGorrill, Sr.
Deer Isle, Maine

Dave's Note: Some folks don't like the flavor of cooked olives so perhaps you should not include them.

GOURMET MACARONI AND CHEESE

I don't think I've ever made just a single recipe of this—I always double or triple the recipe. It can be made a day in advance and baked the next, and it also freezes well. Of all my recipes, this is one that has been requested many times. Men love it.

1 cup elbow macaroni
2 cups cream-style cottage
   cheese
1 cup sour cream
1 egg, lightly beaten

¾ teaspoon salt
⅛ teaspoon pepper
2 cups shredded cheddar
   cheese
Paprika to taste

☐ Preheat oven to 350°F.

Cook macaroni according to package directions; drain well and set aside. Combine cottage cheese, sour cream, egg, salt, and pepper in a large bowl, gradually stirring in shredded cheddar cheese. Mix well and add cooked macaroni. Spoon mixture into a buttered 2-quart casserole or 9-inch square baking dish. Cover and bake for about 45 minutes. Uncover and sprinkle with paprika and bake 5 minutes longer.

Makes 6 to 8 servings.

Mrs. Mystery

AUBERGINE À LA PROVENÇALE

My mother created this casserole to sneak her favorite, eggplant, into us as children. Now married, I make it for my own two children, who enjoy it as much as I did. A wonderful companion for fried chicken or chicken Kiev.

2 eggplants (about 1¼ pounds each)
3 teaspoons salt
4 tablespoons olive oil
4 tablespoons butter
3 green peppers, seeded and sliced
3 medium onions, sliced
1 clove garlic, crushed
½ teaspoon pepper
½ teaspoon Italian seasoning
1 can (16 ounces) ground tomatoes
1 pound mozzarella cheese, grated
2 cups seasoned croutons

☐ Preheat oven to 350°F.

Pare and dice eggplant; place in a colander and sprinkle with 2 teaspoons of the salt. Let stand for 30 minutes, then wipe dry with paper towels.

Heat 2 tablespoons of the olive oil and 2 tablespoons of the butter in a large skillet. Sauté eggplant for about 5 minutes. Remove and set aside. Add remaining 2 tablespoons each butter and olive oil to skillet and sauté green peppers, onion, and garlic for about 5 minutes. Carefully spoon eggplant into skillet and add remaining teaspoon salt, the pepper, Italian seasoning, and tomatoes. Mix. Place half of the mixture in a greased casserole and add half of the cheese. Place remaining mixture in casserole and top with the rest of the cheese. Cover with a layer of croutons. Cover with foil and bake for 50 minutes.

Makes 8 servings.

Cindy Marshall
Danvers, Massachusetts

Dave's Note: I snuck in a little more garlic—eggplant is a little bland to my palate.

MOCK OYSTER CASSEROLE

1 large eggplant, pared and
   cut in 1-inch cubes
½ teaspoon salt
18 saltines, crushed
2 eggs, lightly beaten
½ cup milk
1 can (10½ ounces) cream
   of mushroom soup

⅛ teaspoon pepper
1 teaspoon chopped onion
¼ cup minced red or
   green pepper (or ½ cup
   minced celery)
Tabasco to taste
1 tablespoon butter

☐Preheat oven to 375°F.

In a large saucepan, cover eggplant with water, sprinkle with
the salt, and bring to a full boil. Reduce heat and simmer, uncovered, for 3 minutes; drain. Place one-third of the cracker crumbs
in a buttered 2-quart casserole. Top with half of the eggplant and
repeat. Heat milk, soup, pepper, onion, red or green pepper, and
Tabasco in a pan; add slightly beaten eggs. Pour slowly over the
casserole. Liquid should come just to the top of the crackers. Dot
top with butter and cover. Bake for 30 minutes. Uncover and add
more milk, if necessary. Bake, uncovered, for 10 to 15 minutes
longer, until golden brown.

Makes 6 servings.

Mrs. Claire Cabara
Taunton, Massachusetts

EGGPLANT PARMESAN WITH
RICOTTA FILLING

My folks came from northern Italy and my husband's folks came
from Sicily, so I combined both traditions and came up with this
recipe.

1 eggplant
3 eggs, beaten

2 cups flavored bread
   crumbs

Vegetable oil
1 pound (2 cups) ricotta
  cheese
3 tablespoons fine dry
  bread crumbs
2 eggs, beaten

½ cup grated Parmesan
  cheese
Tomato sauce
Grated cheese of your
  preference

☐Preheat oven to 325°F.

Pare and slice eggplant; dip each slice in eggs and then bread crumbs. Fry in about ¼ inch of hot oil until light brown on both sides. Set aside and prepare filling. To make filling, mix ricotta, bread crumbs, eggs, and grated Parmesan.

Line a square baking dish or casserole with tomato sauce. Place 1 tablespoon of ricotta filling on each slice of eggplant and roll like a jelly roll. Place each roll side by side in a baking dish. Cover with more tomato sauce; sprinkle top with grated cheese. Bake, uncovered, for 25 minutes. Serve hot.

Makes 6 to 8 servings.

Mary Louise Maniscalco
Framingham, Massachusetts

LEGUMES À LA NAPOLITANE

¾ cup finely chopped
  onion
2 tablespoons minced
  garlic
3 tablespoons olive oil
3 cups peeled, cubed
  (1-inch) eggplant
2 cups cubed (1-inch)
  zucchini

2 sprigs fresh thyme or 1
  teaspoon dried thyme
1 bay leaf
1½ cups chopped tomatoes
4 slices mozzarella cheese
2 tablespoons grated
  Parmesan cheese
Salt and pepper to taste

☐Preheat oven to 400°F.

Sauté onion and garlic in hot oil until soft. Add eggplant, zucchini, thyme, and bay leaf; sauté for 5 minutes. Add tomatoes, then spoon mixture into a baking dish and cover with mozzarella. Sprinkle with Parmesan. Place the baking dish on a baking sheet to catch drippings. Bake, uncovered, for 10 minutes. Makes 4 servings.

Anne Depoian
Chelmsford, Massachusetts

COMPANY SQUASH CASSEROLE

1 pound yellow summer
   squash, cut in ¼-inch
   slices
1 medium onion, cut in
   ¼-inch slices
Salt
3 tablespoons butter
3 tablespoons all-purpose
   flour

1 cup milk
1 cup shredded American
   cheese
1 can (3 ounces) sliced
   mushrooms
½ cup soft fresh bread
   crumbs
¼ cup chopped pecans

☐Cook squash and onions, uncovered, in boiling, salted water until tender, about 6 to 8 minutes. Drain and set aside. In a separate pan, melt 2 tablespoons butter over low heat and gradually stir in flour. Add milk, stirring constantly, and cook until thick and bubbly. Add cheese and mushrooms. Stir until cheese melts. Arrange half of the squash and onions in a greased 1½-quart casserole dish and cover with half the sauce. Repeat, cover, and chill in refrigerator.

Toss bread crumbs, pecans, and remaining 1 tablespoon butter, melted, in a small bowl and chill in refrigerator.

Preheat oven to 350°F.

Bake squash, covered, for 25 minutes. Sprinkle top with pecan mixture and bake, uncovered, for 20 to 25 minutes longer. Makes 6 to 8 servings.

Hazel M. Pierce
Black Mountain, North Carolina

SUMMER SQUASH CASSEROLE

2 cups cooked, mashed
  squash
½ cup mayonnaise
1 tablespoon chopped
  onion
1 egg, beaten
1 tablespoon sugar

1 cup grated cheese of
  your choice
4 tablespoons butter
Salt and pepper
Buttered bread crumbs or
  cornflakes

☐Preheat oven to 350°F.

Mix all ingredients except crumbs. Place in a greased casserole dish and top with crumbs. Bake for 30 minutes.

Makes 4 servings.

Helen Elliot
Jaffrey, Massachusetts

CRUNCHY ZUCCHINI CASSEROLE

2 beef or chicken bouillon
  cubes
2 cups boiling water
3 tablespoons butter or
  margarine
1 cup bulgur
½ cup minced onion
1 teaspoon dried oregano,
  crumbled

½ teaspoon dried basil,
  crumbled
1 can (8 ounces) tomato
  sauce
½ pound zucchini, thinly
  sliced
1 cup cottage cheese
½ cup grated Parmesan
  cheese

☐Grease a 2-quart baking dish. Add bouillon cubes to boiling water, stirring until dissolved. Melt butter or margarine in a large skillet over medium-high heat. Add bulgur and onion and sauté, stirring, until onion is tender, about 10 minutes. Blend in bouillon, oregano, and basil. Cover and bring to a boil. Reduce heat and simmer until liquid is absorbed, about 15 minutes. Stir in tomato sauce and zucchini. Cover and simmer, stirring occasionally, until zucchini is crisp-tender, about 15 to 20 minutes.

Preheat broiler.

Turn zucchini mixture into broiler-proof baking dish. Spoon cottage cheese evenly over top, then sprinkle with Parmesan cheese. Broil 4 inches from heat source until top is lightly browned, about 3 to 5 minutes. Serve immediately.

Makes 6 to 8 servings.

Dave's

ZUCCHINI CASSEROLE

4 medium zucchini, cut in
   ¼-inch slices
¾ cup shredded pared
   carrots
½ cup minced onion
6 teaspoons butter or
   margarine

2½ cups herb stuffing
   cubes or seasoned
   croutons
1 can (10½ ounces) cream
   of chicken or mushroom
   soup
½ to 1 cup sour cream

☐ Preheat oven to 350°F.

Cook zucchini in boiling water until tender, about 6 to 8 minutes. Drain and set aside. Sauté carrot and onion in about 4 teaspoons of the butter until tender. Remove from heat and stir in 1½ cups stuffing cubes or croutons, the soup, and sour cream to taste. Gently stir in zucchini and place mixture in a greased casserole. Melt remaining butter to coat remaining stuffing cubes or croutons and spread on top of casserole. Bake, uncovered, for 30 to 40 minutes.

Makes 8 servings.

Lynne McGrane
Danvers, Massachusetts

BROCCOLI CASSEROLE
(With Beef)

I tote this everywhere—brunches, pot luck suppers, buffets—and always receive raves! By the way, it's yummy with leftover chicken and also turkey. This is one of those girls-get-together-trade-recipes things. I've used it for roughly six years or so. Can you imagine our mothers having all these convenience foods and turning out such a nourishing meal? Watch it disappear!

1 head broccoli
1 pound ground beef
1 small onion, chopped
1 can (10½ ounces) cream
   of mushroom soup
1 can cheddar cheese or
   cream of celery soup

1 to 2 cups packaged
   stuffing
Cheese (whichever is your
   favorite), sliced

☐Preheat oven to 350°F.

Boil or steam broccoli until tender-crisp. Brown beef with onion. In the above order, layer all the ingredients in large casserole dish. Cover and bake for approximately 45 minutes.

Makes 4 servings.

Mrs. Sylvia A. Gallant
Melrose, Massachusetts

Dave's Note: A very hearty and filling dish, but I would barely or not cook broccoli before baking for more crunchy texture.

BROCCOLI CASSEROLE

A few years ago, I made this casserole for some friends who were having a family gathering, and I delivered it to their house, leaving it with the other dishes that were collecting on the table. A short time later, I phoned my friends and advised them to be sure and serve it bubbly hot, but they informed me that the guests had not only devoured it without waiting for it to be heated, but they had all asked for the recipe.

2 medium onions, chopped
3 tablespoons vegetable oil
1 package frozen (10 ounces) chopped broccoli, thawed
⅓ cup milk

1 jar (8 ounces) processed cheese spread
1 can (10½ ounces) cream of chicken soup
3 cups cooked rice

☐Preheat oven to 350°F.

In a large skillet, sauté onions in hot oil until soft. Add thawed broccoli, milk, cheese spread, and soup. Cook over low heat until thoroughly mixed and heated through. Stir in cooked rice and place mixture in a buttered casserole dish. Bake, uncovered, for 25 to 30 minutes.

Dorothy Mitchell
Scituate, Massachusetts

CAULIFLOWER AND BROCCOLI CASSEROLE

Almost every time I'm invited out to dinner I am asked to bring this casserole.

1 bunch broccoli, cut up
1 head cauliflower, cut up
2 cans onion rings
1 can (10½ ounces) cheddar cheese soup

½ can (13-ounce size) evaporated milk
Salt and pepper to taste

☐Cook broccoli and cauliflower until half done (you can steam or boil). Place florets and stalks in the bottom of a casserole dish. Layer one can of onion rings on top of vegetables. Beat together soup, milk, salt, and pepper. Pour over vegetables. Top with remaining can of onion rings. Bake uncovered, for about 20 to 25 minutes.

Makes 8 servings.

Mrs. Anna Curis
Millville, Massachusetts

GREEN AND WHITE VEGETABLE BAKE

2 tablespoons corn-oil margarine
½ pound cauliflower, broken into florets, stems peeled and cut into ½-inch pieces
½ pound fresh broccoli, broken into florets, stems peeled and cut into ½-inch pieces
Salt and freshly ground pepper to taste
½ pound carrots, pared and diced

1 small onion, diced
1 large red or green pepper, seeded and chopped
7 eggs
1¼ cups milk
1 pound Monterey Jack cheese, grated
1½ teaspoons minced garlic
1 to 2 tablespoons soy sauce
1 teaspoon celery seed
½ teaspoon dillweed

☐Melt margarine in a medium skillet until foam subsides. Add cauliflower and broccoli *stems*, salt, and pepper. Cook over low heat for about 5 minutes, stirring occasionally. Add carrots, onion, peppers, and cauliflower and broccoli *florets*. Cover and cook until tender, about 10 minutes, stirring occasionally.

Preheat oven to 350°F.

Beat eggs and milk in a large bowl. Add cheese, garlic, seasonings, and vegetables. Turn into a lightly greased deep, 3-quart baking dish. Place baking dish in a large shallow pan filled to 1-inch depth with boiling water. Bake until knife inserted in center of casserole comes out clean, about 50 to 60 minutes.

Makes 6 to 8 servings.

Dave's

SWEDISH CAULIFLOWER

½ head cauliflower,
    broken in buds
2 slices bread
2 teaspoons prepared
    mustard

2 tablespoons sharp cheese
    spread
1 egg
1½ cups milk, or as needed

☐ Cook cauliflower for 8 to 10 minutes (should be firm) in boiling water. Spread bread with mustard and cheese spread. Place 1 slice in bottom of greased casserole dish with spread side up. Layer cauliflower over the bread. Place remaining slice, spread side down, on cauliflower. Cover with about 1 cup milk. Let stand for 24 hours in refrigerator. Add more milk if too dry.
    Preheat oven to 350°F.
    Beat 1 egg into ½ cup milk. Pour mixture over top. Bake, uncovered, for 45 minutes or until puffy and browned on top.
    Makes 4 servings.

Marguerite Gardiner
Windsor, Ontario, Canada

BAKED BEANS

This recipe for baked beans has been eaten by our family for years. It has drawn "raves" from church suppers, etc., as well as from our own family. The recipe can be made with any type of beans—pea, kidney, yellow eye, soldier, and Jacob's cattle beans.

2 pounds dried beans
2 medium onions,
    quartered
¼ pound salt pork
1 tablespoon salt

1 tablespoon dry mustard
¼ cup (packed) brown
    sugar
¼ cup molasses
⅛ teaspoon pepper

☐ Pick over beans, cleaning out any foreign matter, small stones, bits of dirt, etc. Rinse twice and soak overnight in a kettle, leaving at least a full inch of water over the beans, as they will swell.

In the morning, preheat oven to 300°F.

Pour liquid off beans into a small pot and bring to a boil. In a separate pot (bean pot or any metal kettle) place salt pork, scored both ways, and onions. Pour in three-quarters of the beans and add the salt, mustard, sugar, molasses, and pepper. Top with the rest of the beans; cover with boiling liquid and bake for 7 hours, leaving pot cover ajar. Replenish liquid in pot about every 2 hours, and for the last hour leave the cover off completely to brown.

Makes 10 to 12 servings.

Mr. Sibley A. Lenfest
Malden, Massachusetts

THREE-BEAN CASSEROLE

1 can (6 ounces) cut green beans
1 can (6 ounces) cut yellow wax beans
1 can (6 ounces) baby lima beans
1 jar (6 ounces) baked beans
8 slices bacon
½ cup chopped onion
1 tablespoon dry mustard
1 tablespoon Worcestershire sauce
1 teaspoon salt
½ cup catsup
½ cup (packed) brown sugar
3 tablespoons vinegar

☐Preheat oven to 350°F.

Pour all beans in a shallow glass baking dish. Fry bacon until crisp; remove, crumble, and set aside to drain. Sauté onion in as much bacon grease as necessary. Pour sautéed onion and grease over beans. Mix mustard, Worcestershire sauce, salt, catsup, sugar, and vinegar in a small bowl and pour over beans. Top with crumbled bacon. Bake, uncovered, for 30 minutes.

Mrs. Jeanette Wicherts
Sterling, Illinois

GRINGO CABBAGE

1 medium head cabbage,
    cored
1½ teaspoons salt
⅓ cup butter
3 tablespoons all-purpose
    flour
1½ cups milk

⅛ teaspoon cayenne
    pepper
1 onion, thinly sliced
1 cup grated Parmesan
    cheese
1 cup buttered bread
    crumbs

☐Preheat oven to 350°F.

Coarsely chop cabbage and place in pot; sprinkle with 1 teaspoon of the salt. Cover with boiling water and boil for 7 minutes.

While cooking, prepare white sauce. Melt butter over low heat. Gradually add flour, stirring constantly. Add milk and stir constantly until thick. Add remaining ½ teaspoon salt and cayenne pepper.

Drain cabbage well. Place half of cabbage in a greased rectangular baking dish. Add half the onion slices. Pour half of the white sauce over the cabbage and onion. Sprinkle with half of the Parmesan cheese and half of the buttered bread crumbs. Top with the remaining cabbage and onion and sprinkle with remaining Parmesan cheese and bread crumbs. Bake, uncovered, for 30 minutes.

Mrs. Marion G. Taft
Uxbridge, Massachusetts

BORSCHT-STYLE CASSEROLE

2 pounds beef short ribs,
    cut up
1 tablespoon vegetable oil
    (I use peanut oil)
2 cups sliced pared carrot
1½ cups turnip strips

1 cup sliced celery.
1 cup sliced onion
5 cups water
1 can (6 ounces) tomato
    paste
1 tablespoon salt

¼ teaspoon pepper
1 tablespoon sugar
1 tablespoon vinegar
2 cups fresh beet strips

1 small head cabbage,
    cored and cut in 6
    wedges
Sour cream

☐Preheat oven to 350°F.

In a 4½-quart Dutch oven, brown ribs in hot oil. Drain off excess fat. Add the carrot, turnip, celery, and onion. Blend together 4 cups of the water, the tomato paste, salt, and pepper. Pour over vegetables in Dutch oven. Cover and bake for 2 hours.

Remove from oven and skim off fat. Combine remaining 1 cup water, the sugar, and vinegar, and add to meat mixture. Add beet strips and place cabbage wedges on top of mixture, pushing partially into liquid. Cover and continue baking for 1½ hours more. Pass sour cream to spoon atop each serving.

Makes 6 servings.

Mary A. Lukis
Walpole, Massachusetts

AMISH CABBAGE WITH SOUR CREAM
AND BACON

½ pound bacon, sliced
1 head cabbage, cored and
    sliced
2 small carrots, pared and
    chopped
2 large potatoes, pared and
    thickly sliced

2 tablespoons all-purpose
    flour
1¾ cups boiling water
Salt and freshly ground
    pepper to taste
Dash of cider vinegar
1 cup sour cream

☐Fry bacon until crisp, then drain and pour nearly all of the fat out of the pan. Set bacon aside. In the remaining fat, mix cabbage, carrots, and potatoes. Sprinkle with flour and add the boiling water, salt, pepper, and vinegar. Cover and cook slowly for

50 minutes. When ready to serve, place cabbage and potatoes in a casserole dish and top with sour cream and crumbled bacon. Makes 6 servings.

Eileen Hackett Deveau
Mansfield, Massachusetts

CABBAGE STROGANOFF

1 large head cabbage,
   cored and slivered
1 teaspoon salt
2 tablespoons butter

1 tablespoon vinegar
1 tablespoon sugar
1 cup sour cream

☐ Preheat oven to 350°F.

Boil slivered cabbage in salted water, tightly covered, for 5 minutes. Drain. Place hot cabbage in a greased casserole dish. Toss with butter. In a separate bowl mix vinegar, sugar, and sour cream together and pour over cabbage. Toss well. Bake, uncovered, for approximately 30 minutes.

Makes 4 servings.

Mrs. Charles Dellerman
West Chester, Ohio

HERBED SPINACH BAKE

2 packages (10 ounces
   each) frozen chopped
   spinach
1 cup cooked rice
1 cup grated sharp
   American cheese
2 eggs, lightly beaten
3 tablespoons butter or
   margarine, softened

⅓ cup milk
2 tablespoons chopped
   onion
½ teaspoon
   Worcestershire sauce
1 teaspoon salt
¼ teaspoon dried
   crushed rosemary or
   thyme

☐Preheat oven to 350°F.

Cook and drain spinach. Mix with all of the remaining ingredients. Pour mixture into a buttered 10 × 6 × 1½-inch baking dish. Bake for 20 to 25 minutes, or until knife inserted in the center comes out clean.

Makes 8 servings.

Rebecca Robertson
Thomaston, Maine

UNCLE STEVE'S CASSEROLE

Delicious and healthy.

2 cups chopped Swiss chard
1 clove garlic, chopped or pressed
1 cup brown rice

Salt and pepper to taste
1 cup shredded cheddar cheese
4 tablespoons butter

☐Preheat oven to 350°F.

Cook Swiss chard with garlic until tender. Set aside.

Cook brown rice according to directions. Season with salt and pepper. In a 2-quart casserole dish place layers of rice, Swiss chard, butter, and cheese. Layer until all the ingredients are used. Place some of the shredded cheese on top. Bake, in covered casserole dish, for 40 minutes. Uncover and bake for another 5 to 10 minutes.

Makes 4 to 5 servings.

Stephen Furbish
Saugus, Massachusetts

HASH BROWN CASSEROLE

2 packages (16 ounces
    each) frozen hash brown
    potatoes
2 cans (10½ ounces each)
    potato soup
1 cup sour cream

½ pound grated, sharp
    cheddar cheese
½ teaspoon garlic salt
½ cup Parmesan cheese
2 tablespoons butter

☐Preheat oven to 350°F.

Mix potatoes, soup, sour cream, cheddar cheese, and garlic salt together in a large mixing bowl. Pour into a buttered 2½-quart casserole dish or 13×9-inch baking dish. Dot with butter and sprinkle with Parmesan cheese. Bake, uncovered, for 1 hour.

Makes 8 servings.

Ellen C. Pridham
New Castle, New Hampshire

GOURMET POTATO BAKE

1 cup shredded cheddar
    cheese or 6 ounces
    American cheese slices
7 tablespoons butter
1 cup sour cream
⅓ cup chopped onion

1 teaspoon salt
¼ teaspoon pepper
8 medium potatoes,
    cooked, peeled, and
    diced

☐Preheat oven to 350°F.

Melt cheese and 5 tablespoons of the butter in a saucepan over low heat. Add sour cream, onion, salt, and pepper. Place cooked potatoes in a greased 2-quart baking dish. Pour cheese sauce over potatoes and dot with remaining 2 tablespoons butter. Bake for 35 minutes.

Makes 8 servings.

Carrie Phelps
Hillsboro, New Hampshire

SWEET POTATO WITH CINNAMON AND CITRUS SAUCE

Delicious served with ham.

2 large (or 3 medium)
sweet potatoes or yams
6 tablespoons butter or
margarine
2 large (or 3 medium)
cooking apples
3 tablespoons brown sugar

⅓ cup orange juice
1 tablespoon fresh lemon
juice
½ teaspoon cinnamon
½ teaspoon salt
Chopped almonds
(optional)

☐ Scrub sweet potatoes and scrape off woody portion (do not peel). Cook, covered, in salted boiling water for 20 to 30 minutes, until tender.

Preheat oven to 350°F. Butter deep pie plate with 2 tablespoons of the butter.

Drain and peel potatoes. Cut crosswise in ½-inch slices. Pare and slice apples (about ¼ inch). Make layers of potatoes and apples, slightly overlapping.

In a saucepan, melt remaining 4 tablespoons butter; stir in the sugar, orange and lemon juices, cinnamon, and salt. Pour sauce over potatoes and apples. If desired, sprinkle with chopped almonds. Bake, uncovered, for 25 to 30 minutes, or until apples are tender. Baste a couple of times while baking and before serving.

Makes 6 to 8 servings.

D. Eileen Duffy
Somerville, Massachussetts

Dave's Note: Very much a treat.

SWEET POTATO AND BANANA CASSEROLE

4 pounds sweet potatoes
1 teaspoon salt
6 medium bananas (about
2½ pounds)
¼ cup orange juice

½ cup light brown sugar
½ teaspoon ground
cinnamon
4 tablespoons butter or
margarine

☐Wash sweet potatoes. Place in a large saucepan; cover with boiling water and add salt. Bring to a boil and reduce heat; simmer, covered, for 30 to 35 minutes, or until tender. Drain potatoes and let cool. Peel and slice crosswise into ¼-inch-thick slices.

Preheat oven to 375°F. Lightly butter a 2-quart soufflé dish or casserole.

Slice bananas ¼ inch thick and toss in a bowl with orange juice. Combine brown sugar and cinnamon in a small bowl. Arrange a third of the potatoes in a single layer, overlapping slightly, in bottom of prepared dish. Top with half of the sliced bananas, overlapping slightly. Sprinkle with a third of the brown sugar mixture and dot with a third of the butter. Repeat layering with half remaining potatoes and remaining bananas (reserve 12 slices). Sprinkle with half remaining brown sugar and dot with half remaining butter. Repeat layering with remaining potatoes around inside edge of the dish. Arrange 12 banana slices in center to look like a flower. Sprinkle with remaining sugar and dot with remaining butter. Bake, uncovered, for 45 minutes, or until bubbling hot.

Makes 12 servings.

Dave's

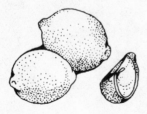

FINNISH TURNIPS

Some people, especially the young, do not like the taste of turnip. This dish camouflages it; the taste is delicious. The recipe is from Finland.

3 cups cooked, mashed
    turnip
Salt and pepper to taste
Pinch of sugar
2 tablespoons butter

½ cup milk
1 egg
Nutmeg
¾ cup crushed
    cornflakes

☐Preheat oven to 300°F.

Into a blender or a large bowl, put turnip, salt and pepper, sugar, butter, milk, egg and a sprinkle of nutmeg. Blend or beat well. Turn into a buttered mold. Cover with crushed corn flakes and dot with butter. Bake for 1½ hours.

Makes 4 servings.

Jeanne Hansen
Waltham, Massachusetts

FINNISH TURNIP CASSEROLE

4 tablespoons butter,
    melted
½ cup farina or cream of
    wheat
2 eggs
⅔ cup evaporated milk
2 tablespoons sugar
⅓ teaspoon salt

Pinch of pepper
⅛ teaspoon nutmeg
⅛ teaspoon ground
    cinnamon
2 cups cooked, mashed
    yellow turnip
2 tablespoons butter, cut
    up

☐Preheat oven to 350°F.

Add melted butter, farina, eggs, milk, sugar, and spices to mashed turnip. Pour into a 1-quart casserole, dot with the 2

tablespoons cut-up butter and bake for at least 1 hour or a little longer, until top is browned.
Makes 4 servings.

Mrs. Vieno S. Kelly
Fitchburg, Massachusetts

MUSHROOM SOUFFLÉ

½ pound "creamed sharp cheddar" cheese
1 cup *uncondensed* cream of mushroom soup
4 eggs, separated

Salt and pepper to taste
¼ cup crumbled cooked bacon
¼ cup sliced blanched almonds

☐Preheat oven to 350°F.

Slowly melt cheese in top of double boiler over simmering water. Add soup gradually, stirring constantly. When well blended, slowly add beaten egg yolks, stirring constantly. Cook slowly until slightly thick. Season to taste and remove from heat.

Beat egg whites stiff, then fold in to egg yolk mixture. Pour into a greased casserole dish and sprinkle with the bacon and almonds. Bake, uncovered, for 1 hour.

Ruth Beeman
Quincy, Massachusetts

CORN CASSEROLE

6 strips bacon
1 medium onion, chopped
1 cup cut-up Swiss cheese
2 cans (16 ounces each) cream-style corn

2 eggs, beaten
½ cup condensed milk
¼ teaspoon chili powder
¼ teaspoon salt
¼ teaspoon pepper

☐Preheat oven to 350°F.

Cook bacon until crisp; drain, cool, and crumble. Pour out all but 2 tablespoons of the drippings and sauté onion. Cut cheese into small pieces. Combine corn, cheese, bacon, onion, beaten eggs, milk, and seasonings and pour into a greased casserole dish. Sprinkle top with a little more chili powder. Bake, uncovered, for 45 minutes.

Dorothy Lainez
Sudbury, Massachusetts

STEWS

Some stews really stick out in my mind. The first one in which I had a hand was on a camping trip to North River, which is just above North Creek, which is just above Glen Falls, which is just above Albany, New York. Well, anyway, Ted Herlyn and I were in charge of our initial meal out under the stars, and it was important because our diet to that point had consisted of bologna and bread, nothing else. Bologna and bread.

This stew started with a mild argument. How big was a "bite-sized" piece? My mother's recipe for "hearty" (weren't they *all*?) called for bite-sized pieces. We discussed bite size according to my mouth or his and he really had a big mouth! We came up with a fantastically brilliant solution. In order to be sure each piece was exactly right, we bit the carrots, potatoes, even the onions. We cut nothing, we bit. Looking back, I can easily remember how difficult it was when we got to the meat. Tough! God, was it tough! Do you know how difficult it is to saw raw meat with your teeth when you're laughing so hard you hurt? Ask me how the stew was. How would it be when you thicken it with Cream of Wheat because you have no flour? We also snuck in two cans (small) of string beans for laughs. They sure did look funny—two nice, shiny, unopened cans in that bubbling stew pot!

In Lisbon, Portugal, there is a unique restaurant. Well, I thought so because all the waiters wore formal wear even at lunch, and they were all thirteen years of age or under. Wait a minute, I forgot—one was fourteen. He was the headwaiter.

Truthfully, the service was quick, efficient, and gracious—as good as I've ever experienced anywhere.

After some excellent fish soup, we were served a stew entrée. It was super. A rich, dark sauce with lots of meat and vegetables. The veggies I could identify, but the meat and resulting gravy, I could not. Knowing something about cuisine, I realized that the chef had concocted some miracle marinade for his beef, and I was determined to get the recipe.

My waiter, who was twelve, patiently listened to me pose the question to my interpreter as to the makeup of the gravy, then asked, in perfect English, "Would you like to know why your lunch was so delicious?"

I said, "Yes. Are there any secret ingredients? Was the meat beef or veal?"

He answered that the cook was very well known for his spicy sauces, which contained many herbs and spices—and, by the way, the meat was dog.

"Dog?" I said.

"Only the best dog," he said. *"Dog?"* I said. By now, I detected an ache in my stomach. My head was reeling a bit with thoughts of Muffin, Tuffy, Thurber, Butch, and a couple of others.

I'll never forget that bright-eyed kid, who suddenly smiled the biggest smile I've ever seen and said something to the effect that somebody at our table had put him up to this after watching me wolf down three and a half helpings. I laughed, somewhat. Heh, heh, heh, I can take a joke.

By the way, the meat was goat.

So many people sent in beef recipes (approximately four hundred), but as you can see, I've whittled that down to half a dozen.

TURKEY CACCIATORE

2 tablespoons olive oil or
  vegetable oil
4 pounds turkey thighs,
  drumsticks, or
  hindquarters
3 large onions, chopped

4 cloves garlic, minced or
  pressed
2 green peppers, seeded
  and chopped
½ pound fresh
  mushrooms, sliced

2 tablespoons all-purpose
flour
1 can (8 ounces) tomato
sauce
1 can (16 ounces) whole
tomatoes, drained
½ cup dry red wine
½ cup chicken broth
½ teaspoon salt

1 teaspoon dried basil
1 teaspoon dried thyme
1 teaspoon dried oregano
3 teaspoons sugar
⅛ teaspoon ground
allspice
2 whole bay leaves
⅓ cup grated Parmesan
cheese

☐In a 6- to 8-quart Dutch oven or large frying pan, heat the oil over medium-high heat. Put in the turkey pieces. Cook, turning, until browned all over; remove pieces as they are browned. Add the onions to the pan and cook until limp. Then add the garlic, green peppers, and mushrooms. Cook until most of the juices have cooked away, stirring often. Sprinkle the flour over pan, mixing it in well. Add the tomato sauce, tomatoes (break up into pieces with a spoon), red wine, chicken broth, salt, basil, thyme, oregano, sugar, allspice, and bay leaves. Bring to a boil while stirring.

Return turkey to the pan, pushing pieces down into the sauce. Cover, reduce heat, and simmer for about 30 minutes. Uncover, stir gently, then increase heat, if necessary, to keep mixture simmering. Cook, uncovered, until turkey is tender, about 1 to 1½ hours, stirring occasionally.

Transfer turkey and sauce to a deep platter, first discarding bay leaves, and sprinkle with Parmesan cheese. Serve with parsley-buttered spaghetti. Pass more Parmesan cheese at the table to sprinkle over individual servings.

Makes about 8 servings.

Dave's

Dave's Note: You may substitute ½ cup of broth for the wine.

MOM'S OLD-FASHIONED BEEF STEW

On my grandfather's farm, where seven of us children grew up, Mom had her hands full trying to feed us. There were fourteen at a table at a time. Dad, Mom, Grandpa, four hired hands, and all the children. Mom concocted this stew. It was the one dish we all enjoyed with no complaints. During the growing season, every herb and fresh vegetable found its way into the pot. At that time, Newfoundland was a British colony. When the officers on their way to their barracks would drop in, there was always plenty for everyone. Mom's stew became so well known, neighbors from the West End came for the recipe. The men asked for copies to send back to England.

4 pounds boneless beef
    stew meat, cut into
    1½-inch cubes
4 cups beef stock
12 potatoes, pared and
    quartered
12 carrots, pared and
    quartered
1 pound white onions,
    peeled
3 fresh, ripe tomatoes,
    quartered

1 tablespoon sugar
1 teaspoon salt
¼ teaspoon dried thyme
¼ teaspoon pepper
¼ teaspoon monosodium
    glutamate (optional)
2 bay leaves
1 clove garlic
¼ cup all-purpose flour
½ cup cold water

☐Simmer meat, covered, in beef stock in a large kettle for 1 to 1½ hours, or until tender. Add vegetables and seasonings; simmer, covered, for about 30 minutes longer, or until vegetables are tender. Blend flour with cold water to make a smooth paste. Slowly stir into soup, stirring constantly until thickened.
    Makes 12 servings.

Mrs. William Connolly
Melrose, Massachusetts

BLACK FOREST BEEF STEW

2 to 2½ pounds beef stew
   meat, cut in ¼-inch
   cubes
2 tablespoons all-purpose
   flour, or as needed
2½ teaspoons salt
¼ teaspoon pepper
2 tablespoons lard or
   drippings
2 cups water

⅔ cup vinegar
½ cup (packed) brown
   sugar
1 medium onion, thinly
   sliced
1 large bay leaf
½ teaspoon ground
   cinnamon
⅛ teaspoon ground
   cloves

☐Combine 2 tablespoons flour, the salt, and pepper; dredge beef cubes in enough flour to cover, then sear in lard until brown. Add remaining ingredients. Bring to a boil, stirring to dissolve the sugar. Reduce heat to low, cover tightly, and cook slowly for 1½ to 2 hours, or until meat is tender. It may be necessary to add additional flour at this point if the gravy looks too thin.
   Makes 6 to 8 servings.

Mrs. N. Biltcliffe
Fall River, Massachusetts

OVEN STEW

3 pounds boneless beef, cut
   into 1-inch cubes
3 or 4 carrots, pared
1 can (16 ounces) tomatoes
2 onions, chopped

1 cup red wine
8 small whole potatoes,
   pared
3 or 4 celery stalks
Salt and pepper to taste

☐Preheat oven to 350°F.
   Vegetables may be cut into small pieces if you prefer. Put all

of the ingredients into a casserole dish and cover. Bake for 2 hours, until meat is tender.
Makes 6 servings.

Mary Degnan
Pawtucket, Rhode Island

BEAN POT STEW

1 pound boneless stew
    beef, cut into 1-inch
    cubes
1 onion, sliced or whole
1 can (10½ ounces) tomato
    soup

¼ cup water (rinse out
    soup can)
1 jar (2½ ounces) pitted
    green olives, juice
    included

☐Preheat oven to 325°F.
Bake all the ingredients in a small, covered bean pot until meat is done (usually about 3 hours). Serve with rice or noodles.

Doris Abbott
Buzzards Bay, Massachusetts

Dave's Note: This is quite different and very tasty. The olives are what makes it.

PRAIRIE STEW

3 pounds boneless beef
    chuck, cut into ½-inch
    cubes
3 to 4 tablespoons olive oil
½ cup hominy, drained
2 to 3 fresh, ripe tomatoes,
    peeled, seeded, and
    chopped
1 dried hot red chili,
    seeded and chopped

1 to 2 cups water
1½ to 2 tablespoons
    cilantro (fresh
    coriander), chopped, or
    2 teaspoons dried or
    chopped fresh parsley
Salt and freshly ground
    pepper

☐Preheat oven to 325°F.

In a Dutch oven, brown meat in hot oil, a few pieces at a time. After first batch of meat has browned, remove with a slotted spoon and set aside while you brown the rest. (Do not crowd pot.) Return all of the meat to Dutch oven and add hominy, tomatoes, chili, and about a cup of water, enough to make gravy. Cover and bake until tender, about 2 to 2½ hours. Add more water if necessary. About 15 minutes before cooking is completed, season with cilantro, salt, and pepper.

Makes 6 to 8 servings.

Dave's

FRENCH BEEF STEW

Great served over noodles, rice, or potatoes.

2 pounds boneless beef
   stew meat, cut into
   1-inch cubes
2 beef bouillon cubes
2 onions, chopped
3 tablespoons instant-
   cooking tapioca

4 cups water
2 tablespoons fine dry
   bread crumbs
1 can (3 ounces)
   mushrooms, drained
Salt and pepper to taste

☐Preheat oven to 350°F.

Place all ingredients in a casserole dish or roaster. Cover and bake for 3 hours.

Makes 4 to 6 servings.

Mrs. B. Cryzewski
Toledo, Ohio

FLEMISH BEEF STEW

Beer is the liquid in this subtly herbed stew. Belgian cooks often add a dozen or so whole dried prunes to plump slowly as the meat simmers and to provide a ready-made fruit accompaniment.

⅓ cup all-purpose flour
2½ teaspoons salt
½ teaspoon pepper
2½ pounds boneless stew
   beef, cut into 1-inch
   cubes
3 tablespoons vegetable oil
1½ cups chopped onions
⅛ teaspoon garlic
   powder

1 teaspoon dried thyme,
   crushed
½ teaspoon ground
   nutmeg
1 can (12 ounces) beer
Hot buttered noodles
   (optional)
Snipped fresh parsley

☐Mix flour, salt, and pepper; coat meat with mixture. Heat oil in a Dutch oven or heavy kettle and brown meat slowly and evenly. Stir in onion, garlic powder, thyme, and nutmeg. Add beer. Cover and simmer for about 1¾ hours, or until meat is tender.

If desired, serve over hot buttered noodles. Garnish with parsley.

Makes about 6 servings.

Cathy Gibson
Revere, Massachusetts

Dave's Note: The thyme flavor comes through quite strongly. Two of us liked it; two of us did not. I liked it because it's different.

BOOTHBAY HARBOR BEEF STEW

I found this recipe in a book about seventy-five years old, put out by a local church; but they added three cloves and a small turnip, which I haven't tried yet. In the book it is called a "Dutch oven

stew," but I like "Boothbay Harbor beef stew" better for a name.
If there is no law against doing so, I'll leave that up to you! You
can also cook this in a crockpot.

2 pounds beef stew meat,
   cut into 1-inch cubes
2 tablespoons cooking fat
4 carrots, pared and sliced
1 can (16 ounces) peas,
   undrained
1 large onion, sliced
¼ cup quick-cooking
   tapioca

1 can (16 ounces) tomatoes,
   undrained
½ green pepper, seeded
   and chopped
1 teaspoon Worcestershire
   sauce
Salt and pepper to taste

☐Preheat oven to 250°F.
   Brown meat in a little fat and place with all the ingredients into
a bean pot. Bake, covered, for 5 hours. Keep the cover on the pot
and it shouldn't dry out in the least.
   Makes 4 servings.

Mrs. Verona Paine
Boothbay Harbor, Maine

HUNGARIAN GOULASH

¼ cup vegetable
   shortening
2 pounds boneless beef
   chuck, cut into 1-inch
   cubes
1 cup sliced onion
1 small clove garlic,
   minced
¼ cup catsup
2 tablespoons
   Worcestershire sauce

1 tablespoon brown sugar
2 teaspoons salt
2 teaspoons paprika
½ teaspoon dry mustard
Pinch of cayenne pepper
1¾ cups water
2 tablespoons all-purpose
   flour
¼ cup water
3 cups hot, cooked noodles

☐Melt shortening in a large skillet. Add beef, onion, and garlic; sauté and stir until meat is brown and onion is tender. Stir in catsup, Worcestershire sauce, sugar, salt, paprika, mustard, cayenne, and 1½ cups of the water. Cover and simmer for 2 to 2½ hours.

Blend flour and remaining ¼ cup water; stir gradually into meat mixture. Heat to boiling, stirring constantly. Boil and stir for 1 minute. Serve over hot noodles.

Makes 6 to 8 servings.

Celia Kanter
Brookline, Massachusetts

PEPPERPOT STEW
(Pfeffer-Potthast)

We call this dish "Grossmama Scherer's stew." Yes, this recipe comes from Bohemia. She made it during the wintertime. If you had a sinus cold, it soon vanished. Oh yes, your sinus cavities seem to shrink to an abnormal condition. However, it is sooooooo good. Gesundheit!

Serve with mashed potatoes—and add a pinch or so of nutmeg to the potatoes while mashing. My ancestors have always done this.

2 **pounds beef short ribs**	**Salt**
2 **tablespoons lard**	**Pinch of cayenne pepper**
6 **onions, sliced**	**Generous amount of**
2 **cloves garlic, chopped or**	**freshly ground pepper**
pressed	**Thin slivers of lemon peel**
2 **bay leaves**	1 **tablespoon capers**
4 **whole cloves**	1 **tablespoon all-purpose**
½ **cup stale rye bread**	**flour mixed with 3**
crumbs	**tablespoons of water**
6 **cups water**	

☐Cut ribs into 2-inch lengths. Sauté in lard until nicely browned. Add onions and garlic; cook until soft. Add remaining ingredients, except for flour and water mixture, and simmer, covered, for 2 hours. Add flour and water mixture during the last 10 minutes.

Makes 4 servings.

Mrs. M. Isabella Slifer
New York, New York

FINNISH FARMER'S MEAT STEW

My father came from Finland eighty-seven years ago. Grandma Saksa always made this, my favorite meal, at the farm in Connecticut. My dad was the cook at our house and I learned this dish from him. He once helped me win a gold ribbon, canning peaches for a city-wide school exhibit.

I cook this in the oven at 300 degrees, and also in my crockpot on low and in an electric skillet.

2 pounds boneless meat (lamb, pork, or beef round), cut in 3-inch cubes

4 medium potatoes, pared and sliced

4 medium carrots, pared and sliced

2 medium onions, sliced

2 teaspoons salt

½ teaspoon pepper

2 tablespoons butter

☐Lay the meat on the bottom of a heavy pot. Top with a layer of potatoes, a layer of carrots, and a layer of onions. Sprinkle each layer with salt and pepper. Dot with butter and cook, covered, over very low heat for about 4 hours, until meat is tender.

Makes 4 to 6 servings.

Julie Saksa D'Errico
Worcester, Massachusetts

MURPHY'S STEW

To the best of my knowledge, my aunt concocted this stew. She is deceased. Since her name was Murphy—ergo, the name of the stew. I added my own touches to suit my family's taste buds.

2 pounds boneless stew beef, cut into 1-inch cubes
5 to 6 cups of water
3 large potatoes, pared, cut in chunks
2 onions, cut in quarters
Vegetables as desired

1 can (10½ ounces) tomato soup
2 cans (10½ ounces each) beef gravy
Salt and pepper or ½ package beef stew seasoning mix

☐Simmer beef, covered, in the water until tender, about 1½ hours. Add all of the vegetables, soup, and gravy; heat through. Season to taste or use ½ package seasoning mix.

Makes about 8 servings.

Peg Booth
Waltham, Massachusetts

STIFADO

One of my neighbors, of Greek extraction, was a fine cook. Her name escapes me, but thirty-two years ago she gave me this recipe.

2½ to 3 pounds lean boneless beef, cut in pieces no larger than 1½ inch
½ cup unsalted butter
2 pounds small onions, peeled, or 2 bags (16 ounces each) frozen pearl onions, thawed

Salt and freshly ground pepper to taste
1 can (6 ounces) tomato paste
⅓ cup burgundy, or as needed
2 tablespoons red wine vinegar
1 tablespoon brown sugar

1 clove garlic, mashed	¼ cup dried apricots
1 bay leaf	Hot, cooked noodles
1 stick cinnamon	
½ teaspoon ground cumin	

☐Melt butter in a heavy kettle; add meat and coat with butter. Place onions on top of meat and add salt and pepper. Mix tomato paste, ⅓ cup burgundy, vinegar, and sugar and pour on top. Add garlic and spices, along with apricots, and simmer for 3 hours. If more liquid needs to be added, use wine. Serve on noodles. Makes 8 servings.

Barbara Heinemann
Ballston Lake, New York

MEATLOAF STEW

Guaranteed to make everyone ask, "What's cooking?" It tastes as good as it smells.

2 pounds ground beef	1 cup water
1 cup tomato sauce	2 tablespoons sugar
1 small onion, chopped	2 tablespoons prepared
½ cup fine dry bread crumbs	mustard
1 teaspoon salt	2 tablespoons vinegar
⅛ teaspoon pepper	4 potatoes, scrubbed
1 egg	4 carrots, pared

☐Preheat oven to 350°F.
Mix together the beef, ½ cup of the tomato sauce, the onion, bread crumbs, salt, pepper, and egg and place in a baking dish. Make a sauce by mixing together the remaining ½ cup tomato sauce, water, sugar, mustard, and vinegar in a small bowl. Place

the potatoes and carrots around the meatloaf. Pour sauce over meatloaf mixture and bake for 1½ hours, basting occasionally. Makes 8 servings.

Mrs. Sally Godin
Auburn, Maine

STEWED CHUCK ROAST

1 boneless beef chuck roast (about 4 pounds)
1 large onion, chopped
4 cloves garlic, slivered
1 cup dry red wine
1 cup water
1 can (8 ounces) tomato sauce
2 tablespoons red wine vinegar

1 bay leaf
7 whole allspice
1 cinnamon stick (3 inches long)
1 teaspoon cumin seed
½ teaspoon salt
½ teaspoon pepper
2 to 3 tablespoons chopped fresh mint

☐Preheat oven to 300°F.

Trim excess fat from roast. Heat fat in a frying pan over medium heat until it renders 2 tablespoons; discard remaining fat. Add onion and garlic to pan; sauté until onion is limp. Add all of the other ingredients, except meat and mint.

Place meat in a 15 × 12-inch baking pan, and pour sauce over top. Cover with foil and bake until meat is very tender when pierced, about 3 to 3½ hours.

Put meat on a platter. Pour sauce into a pan and skim fat. Boil sauce rapidly, uncovered, to reduce to 2 cups. Pour over roast and sprinkle with mint.

Makes 8 to 10 servings.

Dave's

BARBADOS PARTY BEEF STEW

3 pounds boneless beef
    chuck, cut in 1-inch
    cubes
3 tablespoons all-purpose
    flour
2 tablespoons vegetable oil
1 can (16 ounces) tomatoes
2 medium onions, sliced
1 teaspoon celery salt

1 teaspoon salt
¼ teaspoon pepper
⅓ cup vinegar
⅓ cup molasses
1 cup water, or as needed
6 carrots, pared and sliced
½ cup raisins
½ teaspoon ground
    ginger

☐Dust beef with flour. Heat oil in a large skillet or Dutch oven
and brown beef in several batches. Put all meat back into the pan
when all of it has been browned. Add tomatoes (do not drain),
onions, celery salt, salt, and pepper. Mix vinegar, molasses, and
1 cup water and add to pan. Cover and simmer until tender,
about 2 hours. Add more water if needed. Stir occasionally. Add
carrots, raisins, and ginger, cover, and simmer until tender,
about 30 to 35 minutes. Serve on rice, plain or with chutney.
    Makes 10 to 12 servings.

Marcelle Erickson
Brockton, Massachusetts

POLISH VEAL STEW

8 pieces of veal shank
1 tablespoon olive oil
1 large onion, chopped
1 clove garlic, minced
½ cup white wine
2 tablespoons catsup
1 tablespoon lemon juice
2 chicken bouillon cubes
1 teaspoon dried oregano
½ teaspoon dried
    rosemary

1 cup water
5 medium potatoes, pared
4 small white onions,
    peeled
5 medium carrots, pared
    and chopped
2 stalks celery, chopped
1 tablespoon chopped fresh
    parsley

☐In a large heavy Dutch oven, brown veal in hot oil. Add onion and garlic; sauté for 5 minutes. Stir in wine, catsup, lemon juice, bouillon cubes, oregano, rosemary, and water. Cover and simmer for 1 hour, or until meat is almost tender. Add remaining ingredients and simmer, covered, for 30 minutes longer, or until meat and vegetables are tender.
Makes 8 servings.

Regina Bell
Dracut, Massachusetts

LAMB STEW I

3 pounds boneless lamb
  neck or shoulder,
  trimmed and cut into 1-
  to 2-inch cubes
2 tablespoons soy sauce
½ cup Madeira or port
4 teaspoons mustard seed
1 teaspoon dried thyme
¼ teaspoon whole
  peppercorns
2 bay leaves

1½ cups chicken broth
1 cup dry red or white
  wine
1½ to 2 pounds small red
  or white thin-skinned
  potatoes, halved
8 to 12 slender carrots,
  pared
3 to 6 small turnips, pared
  and halved
6 to 12 small white boiling
  onions, peeled

☐Place meat in a 5- to 6-quart Dutch oven. Stir in soy sauce and bring to a boil over medium heat; reduce heat, cover, and let the meat simmer in its accumulating juices for about 30 minutes. Remove lid and turn heat to high to boil juices down completely (about 10 minutes). When meat starts to sizzle in its own fat, stir frequently until meat is richly browned. Add Madeira and stir well to free browned drippings, then add mustard seed, thyme, peppercorns, bay leaves, broth, and wine. Lay potatoes, carrots, turnips, and onions on meat. Bring to a boil; cover, reduce heat,

and let simmer for about 1 hour, or until meat and vegetables are
fork-tender.

Makes 6 generous servings.

Dave's

LAMB STEW II

1 large onion, thinly sliced
8 tablespoons vegetable oil
2½ pounds boneless lamb
   shoulder or neck,
   trimmed and cut into
   1½-inch cubes
1¼ cups water, or as
   needed
2 bunches celery

4 cups (1¾ ounces) loosely
   packed fresh mint
   leaves, finely chopped,
   or ½ cup dried
4 cups (2 ounces) loosely
   packed parsley leaves
   (no stems), finely
   chopped
½ cup lime juice

☐In a 5- to 6-quart pan, sauté onion in 2 tablespoons of the oil
over medium-high heat, stirring until the onion is lightly
browned. Add meat and ¼ cup of the water. Cover and cook on
medium-low heat for 30 minutes. Remove lid and cook until
liquid evaporates; stir to brown meat evenly. Add remaining 1
cup water and stir to loosen browned bits from bottom of pan.
Cover and simmer on medium-low heat until meat is just tender
when pierced, about 30 minutes.

Meanwhile, separate celery stalks and wash well, trimming off
ends and leafy tops. With a vegetable peeler, peel backs off stalks
to remove coarse strings. Dry well with a paper towel. Cut stalks
into 2- to 3-inch lengths. Pour remaining 6 tablespoons oil into
a 10- to 12-inch frying pan and place on medium-high heat. Add
about half the celery at a time to make a single layer in the pan.
Fry, turning, until celery is tinged with gold, about 4 minutes.
Partially cover pan with a lid to avoid excessive spattering. Lift
out celery and let drain on a paper towel. (If prepared ahead,
cover and chill meat and celery separately.)

Drain all but 2 tablespoons of oil from the pan. Add mint and parsley and stir until just wilted; remove from heat. Add celery and herbs to meat along with about ½ cup of water if the pan is almost dry. Cover and simmer until meat is very tender when pierced, about 30 minutes longer. Stir in lime juice. Lift meat and celery from pan and arrange on a large rimmed serving platter. Makes 6 to 8 servings.

Dave's

LAMB AND LENTIL STEW

2 cups lentils
1 pound boneless lamb
    shoulder, trimmed and
    cut into 1-inch cubes
1 tablespoon vegetable oil
1 large onion, diced
1 large carrot, pared and
    diced
6 cups water
4 whole cloves
1 small bay leaf

1 to 1½ teaspoons salt
½ teaspoon chili powder
½ teaspoon ground
    cinnamon
1 cup shredded fresh
    spinach, thoroughly
    cleaned
½ cup chopped fresh
    parsley
8 slices lemon

☐Rinse lentils and pick them over. In a large saucepan or Dutch oven, sauté half the lamb at a time in hot oil until lightly browned. Remove from pan and set aside. Pour off all but 1 tablespoon fat and add onion and carrot; sauté for 3 minutes. Add lamb, water, lentils, cloves, bay leaf, salt, chili powder, and cinnamon. Bring to a boil and reduce heat; cover and simmer gently for 1 hour or until lentils and lamb are tender. Just before serving, stir in spinach and parsley and cook for 1 minute. Garnish each serving with a lemon slice. Makes 8 servings.

Dave's

ARMENIAN BLACK BEAN AND LAMB STEW

1½ pounds lean boneless
   lamb stew meat
2 tablespoons vegetable oil
1 large onion, chopped
3 cloves garlic, pressed or
   minced
1 cup chopped green bell
   pepper

5 cups beef broth
1 can (8 ounces) tomato
   sauce
1 can (8 ounces) tomatoes,
   undrained
1 bay leaf
1 cup dried black or kidney
   beans

☐Preheat oven to 350°F.

Trim and discard excess fat from lamb; cut meat into 1-inch cubes. Combine oil and lamb in a 4- to 5-quart ovenproof pan. Sauté over medium-high heat, stirring often, until well browned. Lift out the meat and add onion, garlic, and pepper to pan; cook, stirring, until onion is limp. Add beef broth, tomato sauce, tomatoes with liquid (break up tomatoes with a spoon), and bay leaf.

Pick over beans, then rinse and drain. Add beans and meat to pan. Bring to a boil, cover, and place in oven; bake for 3 to 3½ hours, until beans are tender.

Makes 4 servings.

Dave's

SMOKED SAUSAGE JAMBALAYA

1 pound smoked sausage,
   cut in ½-inch slices
1 pound ground beef
1 medium green pepper,
   seeded and chopped
½ cup chopped green
   onion

5 cloves garlic, minced
1 can (28 ounces) tomatoes,
   drained
½ teaspoon pepper
1 cup long-grain rice
1½ cups water

☐Cook sausage in Dutch oven until browned. Remove from skillet and discard most of drippings. Combine ground beef, green pepper, green onion, and garlic in Dutch oven; cook until beef is browned. Add tomatoes, salt, pepper, and sausage. Cover and simmer for 20 minutes. Add rice and water to meat and vegetable mixture. Cover and cook for 25 minutes, or until rice is tender.

Makes 4 to 6 servings.

M. Bryant
Colonial Beach, Virginia

MY MOTHER'S CREOLE SUPPER

My mother used to make this in south Texas when I was a little girl—almost seventy years ago.

8 slices bacon
1 medium onion, diced
1 medium green pepper, seeded and diced
3 or 4 pods fresh or frozen okra, diced
1 teaspoon all-purpose flour

1 quart fresh or canned peeled tomatoes
Tabasco to taste
Salt and pepper to taste
Hot, cooked rice

☐In a skillet, fry bacon until crisp, then drain on paper towels. Remove all but about 2 teaspoons bacon grease from the skillet, then add onion, green pepper, and okra. Fry until onion is transparent and green pepper and okra are tender. Add flour and stir; add tomatoes. Cook and stir until tomatoes are thickened. Season with salt, coarsely ground pepper, and Tabasco to taste.

Serve immediately in soup bowls over hot rice. Crumble bacon slices on top of each serving.

Makes 4 servings.

Dorothy Phelps
Wichester, Virginia

PUCHERO À LA CASTILIAN

A very nutritious, simple, filling dish. Wine, salad, and a melon completes it perfectly.

1 cup dried white beans or small lima beans
1 pound pork chops in one piece (center cut)
1 onion, chopped

3 potatoes, pared and quartered
1 small head Savoy cabbage, quartered
Salt and pepper to taste

☐Soak beans or lima beans overnight. Next day, place beans in a saucepan. Add the pork chops (all in one piece) and cold water to cover. Bring to a simmer. Cook slowly until the beans are cooked, about 4 hours.

Add onion, potatoes, Savoy cabbage, and salt and pepper to taste. Cook until done, 30 to 45 minutes. Keep water level just covering the ingredients. Add more water if needed. Serve hot.

Leonor Acebo
Quincy, Massachusetts.

Dave's Note: You might want to add a crushed clove of garlic for some flavor, or ¼ teaspoon dried rosemary.

FRENCH CHICKEN STEW

1 broiler chicken (2 to 3 pounds), cut in serving pieces
½ teaspoon salt
¼ teaspoon pepper
¼ cup vegetable oil
2 tablespoons all-purpose flour
1 teaspoon sugar

⅛ teaspoon dried thyme
⅛ teaspoon dried rosemary
2 tablespoons lemon juice
1 can (6 ounces) mushrooms, drained but liquid reserved
½ cup chicken broth
½ cup dry red wine

1 pound baby carrots,
  pared
12 small onions, peeled

Hot, cooked rice or
  noodles

☐Sprinkle chicken with the salt and pepper. Heat oil in a Dutch oven. Add chicken and brown lightly on all sides. Remove chicken and set aside.

Mix together flour, sugar, thyme, and rosemary. Stir into pan drippings to make a smooth paste. Add lemon juice, mushroom liquid, and broth. Bring to a boil, stirring constantly. Add wine, carrots, onions, and mushrooms. Return chicken to pan; reduce heat and simmer, covered, for 30 minutes. Remove cover and continue cooking at a higher heat until most of the liquid evaporates and chicken and vegetables are coated with a rich, thick glaze. Serve over rice or noodles with remaining broth spooned over.

Makes 4 servings.

Bertha Bravos
Danvers, Maine

CAPTAIN HIGGINS' LOBSTER STEW

This recipe was given to me by the captain of a hospital ship in World War II. He was an excellent cook.

1 pound lobster meat,
  cooked
½ cup butter
4 medium onions, finely
  chopped

4 medium potatoes, pared
  and diced
6 cups milk
Salt and pepper to taste

☐Cut lobster meat in small pieces. Put in a soup kettle with butter and cook for 15 minutes. Boil onions in water to cover for 15 to 20 minutes; boil potatoes in a separate pan of water until tender. Add milk to the lobster and bring to a boil. Add onions and water in which they have been cooked and the potatoes, drained. Season to taste with salt and pepper.

Makes 6 servings.

Clarion Mackie
Allston, Massachusetts

SERGEANT BILL'S CLAM STEW

The name "Sergeant Bill's" refers to my Air Force days. I am a retired sergeant after twenty years. This is an original recipe (mine).

1 clove garlic, minced
5 medium potatoes, pared
   and cubed
2 medium onions, chopped
1 medium green pepper
   (optional), seeded and
   chopped
5 stalks celery, cut in
   1-inch slices

5 medium carrots, pared
   and cut in 1-inch slices
2 cans (16 ounces each)
   whole tomatoes,
   undrained
Salt and pepper to taste
1 can (10 ounces) whole
   baby clams, undrained

☐ Parboil all of the vegetables, except tomatoes, by covering with water and cooking until crunchy. Season to taste. After vegetables are cooked, drain off approximately one-third to one-half of the water. Add clams, with juices, and tomatoes, with liquid. Simmer, covered, over low heat for 30 minutes to 1 hour, or until tender but not mushy.

Makes 4 servings.

Bill Wheaton
Sturbridge, Massachusetts

CIOPPINO MEDITERRANEAN

¼ cup chopped green
    pepper
2 tablespoons finely
    chopped onion
1 clove garlic, minced
1 tablespoon vegetable oil
1 can (16 ounces) tomatoes,
    chopped
1 can (16 ounces) tomato
    sauce
½ cup dry red wine

3 tablespoons snipped
    fresh parsley
½ teaspoon dried
    oregano
½ teaspoon dried basil
Salt and pepper to taste
1 pound fish fillets
1 can (7½ ounces) minced
    clams
1 can (4½ ounces) shrimp

☐Sauté pepper, onion, and garlic in hot oil until tender. Add tomatoes, tomato sauce, wine, parsley, oregano, basil, and salt and pepper. Simmer, uncovered, for about 20 minutes. Add fish, clams, and shrimp. Simmer for 30 minutes more.
Makes 8 to 10 servings.

Steve Hill
Cape Elizabeth, Maine

CRAB STEW

4 tablespoons butter,
    softened
3 tablespoons all-purpose
    flour
2 cups hot milk
½ cup heavy cream

3 tablespoons
    Worcestershire sauce
1 tablespoon celery salt
1 can (6½ ounces)
    crabmeat
¼ cup cream sherry

☐Cream butter and flour together in a saucepan until smooth. Gradually add hot milk to mixture and cook slowly until thick.

Blend heavy cream, Worcestershire sauce, and celery salt and add to mixture. Add crab and keep over low heat. Do not boil. At last moment, add sherry and serve.

Makes 4 servings.

Rose Hill
Lowell, Massachusetts

BOATMAN'S STEW

2 pounds firm-fleshed
  whitefish (cod, haddock,
  or halibut)
2 teaspoons salt
2 onions, sliced
¼ cup vegetable oil
1 can (6 ounces) tomato
  paste

3 cups water
¼ teaspoon cayenne
  pepper
¼ teaspoon pepper
1 cup chopped fresh
  parsley
⅓ cup dry white wine
8 slices Italian bread

☐Sprinkle fish with ½ teaspoon of the salt and let stand for 1 hour.

Meanwhile, lightly brown onions in hot oil; pour off fat. Stir in tomato paste, water, cayenne pepper, remaining 1½ teaspoons salt, pepper, parsley, and wine. Simmer for 30 minutes. Add fish and simmer for about 10 minutes more, or just until fish flakes easily with a fork.

To serve, place a slice of bread in each soup bowl and ladle soup over.

Makes 8 servings.

N. Matowylak
Bedford, New Hampshire

VEGETABLE STEW

1 pound green beans, ends
and strings removed
½ pound asparagus
(optional), tough ends
removed
¼ cup olive oil or
vegetable oil
1 large onion, chopped, or
16 green onions
(including tops),
chopped
2 or 3 cloves garlic,
pressed or minced

2 ounces thinly sliced
dry-cured ham such as
serrano, prosciutto or
Westphalian, finely
chopped
1 package (9 ounces) frozen
artichoke hearts, thawed
1 cup frozen baby lima
beans, thawed
Salt and pepper to taste

☐In a 5- to 6-quart pan, bring 2 to 3 quarts of water to boiling
point. Add green beans and boil, uncovered, for 1 to 2 minutes.
Add asparagus, if using, and continue cooking until vegetables
are tender when pierced, about 4 to 5 minutes longer. Drain. Cut
asparagus diagonally into ½-inch lengths, beans into 2-inch
lengths. Set aside.

Heat oil in the pan; add the onion, garlic, and ham. Sauté,
stirring, over medium heat until onion is soft. Add artichoke
hearts, limas, asparagus, and green beans. Stir until vegetables
are hot. Add salt and pepper to taste. Serve hot or at room
temperature.

Makes 8 servings.

Dave's

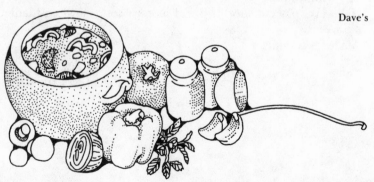

Index